Green writes a powerful narrative abou family — coping with elderly parents, ι can, and connecting with adult children whιιe managing severe illness. Becoming a grown-up (grownupedness) is something we all seek . . . Green, weaving stories from her work as a therapist with personal memories and reflections, helps us get there.

— Elaine Carty, CM, OBC
professor emerita of nursing and midwifery
University of British Columbia

A wonderful read, thanks to the author's superb syntheses of self and other, past and present, personal and professional. The never-ended-ness of grownupedness is everywhere in this savvy interplay of story and insight.

— Sheila Martineau, PhD
writer, copy editor, book designer and researcher
currently writing her memoir of a complicated childhood

As we travel with Green from her earliest memories of childhood in Upstate New York through life's inevitable losses and joys, she reveals a woman who cares deeply about making sense of her well-lived life. As she faces her own end-of-life, she leaves us with the bountiful wisdom gleaned from those labors, as well as a primer for how to confront our own mortality. A book to treasure.

— Rick Gore
retired science editor of *National Geographic*

A deeply compelling conversation on aging and maturity — a marvellous montage of visuals, words and feeling. Reflection, often lost in our seemingly ever-troubled world, is found here. Clarissa's professional knowledge and personal insightfulness push us to reflect on our own stories and those we love.

— Carol Anthony, RN, MSN
retired specialist in gerontology

So far in our efforts to understand aging, we have relied on a host of systematic approaches. Here Green offers us something different. Green takes vignettes from her practice as a family therapist and expands our understanding of how another family can develop their own strategies to resolve a similar issue, and suddenly we have genuinely unique strategies. Further, Clarissa's lean, fresh, and above all personal language supports our learning, and the reader emerges changed.

— JoAnn Perry, RN, PhD
educator and researcher in gerontology

A work that incorporates tenderness and openness, experience and wisdom. Green is a storyteller who reaches out beyond the page to touch the humanity in us all. Seeing the human condition from many vantage points, she has a unique ability to seamlessly weave the professional with the personal. Green, with her poignant questions, insights and skill with the written word, takes us on a thoughtful journey toward grownupedness.

— Sandi Bojm, MSc
counselling therapist and speech language pathologist
specializing in anxiety-related speech disorders

Wise, honest and full of warmth, reading this moving collection of essays means spending time with an insightful and generous writer. A compelling and comforting book. In reflecting on her passage to adulthood and all the trials and tribulations strewn along the way, Green illuminates the path and enlightens everyone about the struggle to grow up. A gutsy examination of family, aging, illness, loss and love.

— Eufemia Fantetti
author of *My Father, Fortune-tellers & Me*
and *A Recipe for Disaster*

Grownupedness

GROWNUPEDNESS

CLARISSA P. GREEN

GRANVILLE ISLAND
PUBLISHING

Publisher's Cataloging-in-Publication Data

Green, Clarissa P., author. Grownupedness / Clarissa P. Green.
Vancouver, BC: Granville Island Publishing, 2020.
ISBN: 9781989467244 (pbk.) | 9781989467251 (ebook)
LCSH Green, Clarissa P. | Green, Clarissa P.—Family. | Family therapists—United States—Biography. | Older people—Family relationships. | Older people—Care. | Adulthood—Psychological aspects. | Aging—Psychological aspects.
BISAC BIOGRAPHY & AUTOBIOGRAPHY / Personal Memoirs | FAMILY & RELATIONSHIPS / Life Stages / General | PSYCHOLOGY / Developmental / Adulthood & Aging | FAMILY & RELATIONSHIPS / Death, Grief, Bereavement

LCC BF724.5 .G74 2020 | DDC 155.6/092—dc23

Cover photo: *Eternal Journey* by Karen Cooper
www.karencoopergallery.com
Author's photo: Signy Novak

Editor: Rebecca Coates
Book designer: Omar Gallegos
Proofreader: Jessica Kaplan

Granville Island Publishing Ltd.
212 – 1656 Duranleau St.
Vancouver, BC, Canada V6H 3S4

604-688-0320 / 1-877-688-0320
info@granvilleislandpublishing.com
www.granvilleislandpublishing.com

Printed in Canada on recycled paper

This book is dedicated
to my sons Chandler and Larson
ever my best teachers

Cover Note

Legacy logs and stumps are common sights in most forests. Also known as nurse logs, the elegant beauty of their decomposition and how the felled wood nourishes new growth and future generations is on artful display. As does the nourishment from a felled tree fuel the future, a family's history similarly flows forward from story, tradition and the wisdom of elders to foster an ongoing unique expression of family.

Contents

Foreword

I can count on one hand the gifted storytellers that I know, and have known, and Clarissa P. Green is among them. Storytelling is our terra firma. Research over the past couple of decades repeatedly confirms that storytelling is far more persuasive than fact-based narratives. Stories take up residence in us; fact-based narratives do not. Research confirms that facts and persuasive-based narratives seldom "stick."

As a young girl, Green knew she was irresistibly drawn to storytelling. This isn't a skill one learns but rather, a role and skill one inherits. When Green's elderly great aunt (who was the consummate family storyteller) informs her that she would be the next family storyteller, she understood. Although the onerous responsibility of the role was daunting, she felt deeply recognized. Ever since, Green has collected, recorded in journals and letters, and recreated these stories in her creative writing.

I met Clarissa P. Green in The Writer's Studio at Simon Fraser University in 2007. She had been accepted into the poetry mentor group; I was on faculty and directing the program. I was struck by her passion for writing then and subsequently struck by her devotion to doing the hard-hard work to bring a piece to fruition which always requires years to do. Bette Davis famously said, "Getting old ain't for sissies!" The same could be said for writing.

A few years after The Writers' Studio, I had the pleasure of working with Clarissa on her nonfiction manuscript. She wrote prodigiously. She had a remarkable cache of stories to tell. This early manuscript was an unusual mix of professional and personal inter-related narratives. It was groundbreaking. For me, when reading a number of these stories once again in *Grownupedness*, it was pure pleasure to see how they have evolved over the years.

In *Grownupedness*, Green speaks directly to us. She skillfully circumvents binary ways of knowing and telling, moves seamlessly in and out of personal storytelling and related professional vignettes of struggling clients. Clients in their early 90s overwhelmed by their own diminishing abilities, and clients who are their elderly "children" vexed by how to navigate their own diminishing vigor, professional and familial demands as they care for a needy parent.

Over and over we are on the edge of our chair in the room with Green and her client(s), or in the car or bedroom with her struggling mother, or in the ER with Green's own serious health crisis and son quietly by her side. In this close-up proximity we witness: when the heart opens, the mind opens to new understanding, new ways of being that enable compassion for oneself, and for one another.

This book is a radical act. There is no turning away or tuning out either side or perspective in these stories. It refuses to extract the story out of the complicated decision-making of old age. Without the possibilities of story, to put it simply, we flounder. Are lost — all of us.

Two of Green's stories: "Driving Lessons" and "Hurricane Days," featuring her very elderly mother and stepfather (riddled with dementia) are utterly unforgettable. Poignant and humorous, this is Green at her zenith of storytelling. These are stories that I will reread again and again over the remaining years of my life. There are, indeed, many such stories in *Grownupedness*. Green's "cast" is rich, all encompassing, and her evolving relationship with her two sons is touching; inspiring.

Clarissa has always been an avid reader and I believe that this — her own book — will attract an equally avid readership.

— Betsy Warland
author of *Lost Lagoon/Lost in Thought*
(published 2020)

Part One

Anatomy of a Crisis

Mom. Father. Sister. Brother. Grandmother. Grandfather. Dog. Tricycle.

Snip. Snip. Snip. Curve scissors around, carefully. Snip.

As soon as I could manoeuvre scissors, I grew fascinated, used my new skill to carefully cut on dotted lines to release paper dolls from booklets Mom bought me. Pages of people, clothes, pets, toys, furniture. After I cut out a family, I dressed them, laid them out side by side on the blue carpet in my bedroom.

Mom also gave me Sears catalogues and old magazines. In those pages, aunts, uncles, cousins, a school and teacher, friends, cars, dolls, a church, a mountain, a streetcar.

"There."

Then, "Once upon a time . . ."

When my six-year-old story line wandered beyond the figures between my knees on the floor — as it had when my next sister was born a year before — I searched for what

I needed to illustrate the story unfolding: baby, bassinette, stroller, babysitter, new doll. Began to carefully cut again. "That's better. Now, everything is all right . . . all over again!"

Upheaval made me search for what would make everything feel okay again; I needed to feel safe, or I felt afraid, hesitant, wanted to run, hide. I sifted through what people, groups, places could make me feel more stable.

Because I'd been able to figure this out so far, I didn't yet know what happened if I couldn't.

That happened when I was nine years old.

Then, after the birth of my youngest sister, Maudie, the eighth child, my family couldn't rebalance. Everything felt tangled, crazy. Everyone seemed stiff and silent, or all over the place and noisy. Mom and Dad made decisions that made no sense to me.

That time was my primer for how crisis emerges when a family can't access what they need to restabilize.

———————

Not long before the summer Maudie was born, my father had a heart attack and was taken away in an ambulance. For months after, he lived at a neighbour's house, not at home. Mom said it was too noisy with seven children and five dogs; Daddy needed *rest*. Then my grandmother also had a heart attack. She took to her bed, stopped visiting.

Maudie stayed in the hospital for all but a few days of her seven-month life. I was told she would die soon, but not why or how.

My parents were forty-three and thirty-eight.

Everything seemed thrown into the air. Breakfast was cereal on the table, get your own bowl and milk. I got to choose my own clothes, no comment from Mom. My older brothers, older sister and I shuttled back and forth to school on the yellow school bus that stopped on the highway at the end of our long driveway. The housekeeper or one babysitter, then another, watched my younger sisters, two and four years old. Supper was often spaghetti and meat sauce. We sat in our places around the Formica table, cracking jokes, Dad's chair empty, Mom's eyes to the side, chewing the side of her cheek.

Mom spent every possible minute at the hospital.

I had no way to explain what was happening, told no one at school about my dying sister, my away-father, my usually ebullient grandmother who now lay in her upstairs bedroom, curtains closed, white hair spread wide on a pillow, no rings on her fingers, eyes closed, silent.

I talked with my dolls, read Lassie stories, but especially I wanted to be close to my mom. I convinced her to pick me up at school, take me to the hospital with her. It felt good to feel the warmth of her leg as I sat next to her on the front seat of the station wagon. While she visited the baby, I waited in the car, listened to the radio. When she returned she turned the radio off, drove slowly, eyes straight ahead. Tears spilled down her cheeks. Over and over, all ten miles up the lake, she mumbled, "Poor darling girl, poor little thing, oh my, oh, oh my." I put one finger on her thigh, stared straight ahead. I had never seen my mom cry before.

Her words seeped into my pores. Her grief became mine.

At home, the sound of piano music, crying and cowboys shooting guns. My older sister was at the piano playing pop songs, as she now did hour after hour. The two little ones were in tears, clinging to the babysitter's legs. The older boys were watching TV, probably to keep Mom from asking too many questions; one had recently been arrested for stealing. Although it was dinner time, the table wasn't set. The babysitter needed to be paid, driven home.

Every day, I worried my mom would die.

After my sister died, there was a funeral. Mom let me choose the yellow knit dress Maudie wore in her small satin-lined coffin. I got to go to the church, stand in line, stare at her. I wanted to touch her face, smaller than some of my dolls. Why would anyone put makeup on a baby?

My parents believed the right way to handle misfortune was to "turn the page." This meant they didn't talk with their children about our sister's death or any of the other awful events around that time. No one asked me or my siblings how we felt.

It was as if no one had feelings, as if that child never existed. In the 1950s, silence was considered an appropriate response to tragedy.

Years later I learned my parents talked about divorce in those months after my sister's death.

What holds a family together when there's that much unexpected change? What can heal a shattered heart, a career ended because of physical frailty, children let loose in not-yet-grown-up lives, a marriage stretched beyond the creativity of a wife and husband?

It's taken me most of my life to understand how this crisis changed my family so profoundly, how it shaped my future. For sixty years I've reviewed those eighteen months, talked with siblings and Mom, would have talked to Dad had he lived long enough.

In my twenties when I was in graduate school, I was drawn to study the ins and outs of family crisis. No awareness of the source of my fascination.

My courses opened me to what causes crisis, how people act and why, how to prevent and effectively intervene to help a family regain balance. Crises, I learned, are part of life. They are rooted in expected milestones — birth, adolescence, marriage, children leaving home, retirement, timely death — and unexpected events — serious illness, accident, love affair, natural disaster, war. Like wind that can blow through or knot into a hurricane, any major event is a potential crisis, because it calls for a family to reorganize, to *change*. Every family member will have a different experience and story, dependent on their age and personal mosaic.

As life accumulates, I learned, so too do milestones and unexpected changes. This gives rise to what might be called a crisis measuring stick. Is this current upsetting time better or worse than previous ones? How is this chaos similar to others? Different? Typically, family members reach toward familiar ways to calm down, feel better. When previous upsets include behaviours that help, chances of crisis lessen. When they increase anxiety and reactivity, they fuel a crisis. Our history follows us around, waiting to be understood, put to work.

During graduate school, I worked for six weeks as a nurse on a unit for premature newborns. Within days I told my supervisor I couldn't stand the tiny bodies lined up in plastic incubators, noisy machines, tubes, gloves, whoosh of oxygen, daily deaths. She asked me what I'd rather be doing, and I looked over to the wide curtained window at the end of the nursery. Outside, parents. On my breaks, I spent time with them. They sat, stood, stared, waited for the drapes to open. "I want to spend time with them."

My supervisor's eyes went wide. "You want to talk with the parents?"

I nodded. She shook her head. This was the 1960s. Grieving was still left on its own, to be silently absorbed or denied.

But what she said was, "If you think you can help those parents, please do. I have no idea what to do with them."

I didn't think about Maudie's short, tragic life, but it must have pushed me to stand by those parents of tiny newborns, watching babies' chests heave up and down, *do something* to be helpful during this time of such fear, sadness and loss.

During the six weeks I spent with those young parents, I used words and actions that might have soothed my own parents as they watched their baby daughter through a window: hands on arms, arms around shoulders, shared silence, gentle interest in a tiny son or daughter, queries about life at home, about feelings.

When Elisabeth Kübler-Ross's books on loss, death and grief were published in the 1970s, I was mesmerized. I understood. The car rides with my mom, especially her sharing her tears and words of sorrow with me, had initiated me into the world of grieving, given me ways to be with people in crisis.

I became a crisis counsellor.

Later, in my forties, as a university professor, again without awareness of the links to my sister's death, I applied for a grant to study the impact on families of the diagnosis of a life-threatening illness in the wife/mother. Side effects of treatment left these women unable to take their usual care of children and husbands. I interviewed families several times over a two-year period about the consequences of the diagnosis and treatments. Families that coped successfully with this potential crisis "imported" a new anchor for the family, often the mother or mother-in-law of the patient, someone who made sure routines remained stable: meals, groceries, dishes, bedtime stories, laundry, housework. Without that mainstay, families cobbled together a daily life that was haphazard. Family members felt on edge, wary, unsafe. Most of those families went into crisis.

This study allowed me to understand the indelible role my mom struggled with in 1954–55, and why we went into crisis. She was our anchor, our manager, our guide; when she turned her energy and time away from her children at home and the running of the household, no one replaced her.

That study also showed me the power of having a replacement anchor during crisis in my own life. The summer I asked my husband to leave, I was a mother of two little boys. I'd not lived in western Canada for long. The closest family member was thousands of miles away. Although I'd made a few friends, they were new in my life. Terrified and weeping, alone in a silent living room, two young children asleep upstairs, feeling crazy, I called my mom.

"I've just ended my marriage, Mom. I'm falling apart, I can't take care of my children. I need you to parent the boys so I can collect my wits. Please, *please* help me."

For a few weeks, my mom did just that.

Mom paid for the boys and me to fly to her home, where we stayed for three weeks. While I slept in, she got up with my two sons, put cereal in their bowls, took them to the beach and the carousel. While I wrote and walked beaches, my mom made my children snacks, put them down for naps, made dinner, read to all three of us. After the boys were in bed, Mom and I sat on her deck, bare feet on a table in front of us, talked, drank Scotch, watched the stars.

Those three weeks not only stabilized my family, they changed everything in my relationship with my mom. Now, we both knew one another's underbellies.

As a family teeters toward a crisis, members reach toward whatever they hope will stop the wobbling, or at least distract from the agony of the upset. Parents discuss and problem-solve, go to church, spend money, drink, talk to friends, become unfaithful, fight, withdraw, hire people to help out, join groups. Children turn to friends or toys or pets; escape in fantasy, books, sex; run away; act out; hide in their rooms; hurt themselves; use alcohol or drugs. But mainly they watch their parents, try to figure out what's going on, worry what will happen to them. In doing so, they use whatever tools they have; often understanding is limited by youth and immaturity, and emotion swamps them.

During the time leading up to and after my sister's death, I'm sure my parents, grandparents, aunts and uncles tried to prevent our daily life from becoming as chaotic as it did. My mom arranged for my father to recuperate for two months at a neighbour's house where it was quiet; we children didn't have to live with the constant admonition *hush*! When it became clear Dad was too frail to ever return to the work he'd done for twenty years, I think my mom's parents offered money to offset his missing salary — a temporary bandage, but not a long-term solution. The people employed to help with housework and maintenance were pulled into child care. Relatives invited us older children to spend the night. When my father was well enough, all children were "farmed out" for two weeks so he and Mom could take a holiday. Despite these efforts, we became a family living on its own edge. My older brothers bullied their younger sisters and experimented with breaking the law. Discipline was unpredictable. While I escaped to fantasy, dolls and books and turned silent at school, my older sister buried herself in music. She and I fought frequently over the territory of our shared bedroom. The two little ones clung, sucked their thumbs, watched for their mom to enter the room. Nothing I could find to cut out of a magazine made the darkness I felt go away. For months, I didn't see Mom smile.

If a family finds and uses enough suitable resources, crisis behaviour typically evens out within a couple of months, sometimes sooner. The pandemonium in my family went on for more than a year.

When our parents returned from their holiday, they reorganized everything we children knew as our life. They announced we would leave family and friends, sell furniture and winter clothing and move to the tropics. We would leave soon. We learned Dad had gone south weeks earlier and bought a house. It was smaller, Dad said, but all three boys would be in boarding school; we wouldn't need so much room.

The next weeks were so swamped with packing, selling seemingly everything, saying goodbye to friends and cousins, there was almost no conversation, even among us children.

Half the family — my father and older siblings — went south by train. I rode with Mom in her blue station wagon with my four- and six-year-old sisters, three dogs, two birds and six African violets. We stayed in motels, listened to the radio, wrestled with maps and stopped to exercise the dogs. My mom drove slowly; she'd never driven more than 100 miles away from home before. We were on the road for a week. I smile when I remember that time.

Miraculously, the move worked.

Even though several older children were adamant nothing about this new plan would work, within six months this life became a welcome exchange for the previous roller coaster ride. Neighbours welcomed us. My older brothers settled into boarding school life. Dad looked for work. My older sister began music lessons. She and I made new friends. My younger sisters made friends who lived on the same street. My mom found a housekeeper to help out three days a week. My parents joined a club, played golf and tennis with other transplants from "the North."

Although the house had little land around it, was tiny compared to our large sprawling house in the North, the tropical climate washed all of us in warm, balmy Atlantic air, scented with salt, hibiscus, oleander, gardenia. We wore sleeveless blouses, had bare legs. Even my father took to wearing Bermuda shorts.

For years I've puzzled over how the move — one more dramatic, major change — finally resolved my family's eighteen-month-long crisis. We left so much behind: the big house and yard; grandparents, aunts, uncles and cousins at Thanksgiving and Christmas; friends; schools; all of us together under one roof.

How could *more turmoil* possibly work?

As a therapist, I know some families end up functioning better after a crisis; others can't even regain who they were beforehand. Theory suggests what makes the difference is the quality and timing of help received. Help that includes a constructive view of the crisis; appreciation for "the story," including what brought on the turmoil; description of how family members are responding; comparison of this crisis with others; connection with people and other resources; structure.

In time I asked my siblings, aging mom and her sisters about this now long-ago crisis more than any other family history event. I needed to understand how Mom and Dad packed up and left behind so many loved ones, holiday rituals and gatherings we children had loved. No two people described the time, or what was important, the same. This astonished me. Still, bit by bit, the falling-apart and putting-back-together emerged.

Mom emphasized the complexity of our large and busy household in New York: so many children, so many others employed to keep everything and everyone going, so much space, yard, distance from town. Dad, she said over and over, "just couldn't do it anymore." "It," I figured out, meant more than his job; it included the complexity, noise level, webs of family, harsh winter weather.

"No one liked the idea. It broke my mom's heart. She got over her heart attack but said she never got over our move," said my mom nodding slowly.

But I knew my mom had a rebel streak. Her sisters agreed. Mom wanted to leave behind mayhem and fear, "try something new," even if that meant leaving family behind. It was time for her and Dad to "start over." For the two of them, Mom made sure we knew, the move was the end of something and the beginning of something else. It was an opportunity. She emphasized how good she and Dad were at making new friends.

As I listened, I realized the move was a project of sorts, one that forced them to work together, create a new chapter, reach out to others — people they had yet to meet — to help. They absolutely believed life would improve — theirs, ours. Did their marriage survive because of her rebel streak?

Even though Dad had to find new work after we moved — and no longer could it be executive work — I never heard a word about money. Not long ago, now sixty years after the move, I came upon letters my father wrote to his sister; they addressed how much less expensive our new life in the tropics was. It was my first real awareness of what it took to finance our lifestyle in New York, how stressful that must have been for him to make all that money. His letters revealed how proud he was to support his family. The crisis brought out his backbone, his desire to take care of his family in different ways.

My older brothers, in disappearing to boarding schools, became visitors for me. Their absence meant the end of teasing, bullying and trickery. For my parents, less noise, worry, fewer discipline problems. For the most part, my brothers enjoyed their boarding school experiences. I've never heard any of them say they wish they could have stayed at home. When they returned for Christmas or Easter holidays, the chaos erupted instantly. While they injected a frisky fun, it was a relief when daily life settled again.

The last time my mom talked about this crisis, she was dying. My older sister, two younger sisters and I had left our own families to live with her for her final several months. We took care of her needs and household, made sure her daily life was as familiar as possible. We four became her anchor. Perhaps that safety allowed Mom's heart to open; we talked about personal issues with more freedom than ever before.

In the midst of a conversation about the ups and downs of Mom's long life, my younger sister asked, "Of all you've been through, Mom, what time was the hardest for you?" She answered almost before the sentence was completed. "It was the year your sister died." She stared off somewhere to the left.

In the previous ten years we'd talked a lot more about the loss of Maudie. I'd participated in a research study focused on the consequences of childhood sibling death, and the interview made me mention my sister's name, talk about the loss, hear how my brothers and sisters and parents were affected. Although initially hesitant, Mom stayed put for the conversations. She began to say Maudie's name.

On my fiftieth birthday my older sister put silverware, plate, wine glass and place card for Maudie on the round table.

"Who's the guest?" asked Mom.

"Look at the place card."

She walked around the table, looked at the four of us, nodded her head, said, "Thank you."

Eight years later as we sat around Mom's deathbed, I said, "Tell me again about Maudie's death. She'd be forty-eight if she were here with us."

Mom reeled off a now-familiar chain of events of 1954–56. We each offered memories and whatever sense we'd made of the loss of this baby and all that happened because of it. I told my familiar story of riding in the car with Mom, how much I needed to be near her, how I tried to be some modicum of comfort.

"My worst nightmare was that you would die too, Mom."

Pause.

Then: "Mom, what made it so truly terribly bad for you?" This was a question I'd not asked her before.

She worried her thumbs, then looked straight at me. "It wasn't just the baby, you know. That was bad enough, but I probably could have handled that, terrible as it was. It was *all three of them*. I spent every day driving from one place to another — my baby, my husband, my mom, all in different places. I never knew who would die first." She worked her jaw, pursed her lips.

Although I'd pondered the crisis, especially the toppling of my strong, capable mother many times, I'd focused on the baby. There'd been no mention at home back then that maybe Dad, maybe Mom's mother, might *die*.

In all my ponderings, I'd never encompassed the profundity of my mom facing the possibility that any or all of the *three* people she loved most in the world could die — at any moment.

––––––––––––––––––

Although this long-ago crisis is not top of my list of "worst I've known," worse than other personal milestones or unexpected events — my divorce, house fire, flood, near-drowning — it's the one with the most pervasive impact. It was the first time I saw my family fall apart, my first encounter with death, loss of predictability, safety, relatives. It left an indelible mark on my priorities, perspective of hard times, curiosity, response to crisis, career — especially career. I kept turning toward what can prevent crisis in other families. How might I foster effective response in times of change?

My work as a therapist to elders and their grown children has allowed me to explore this at close range. Often aging-related milestones upset relationships between old parents and mid-life children; many families seek help. My hope is always to prevent relationships from unravelling, calm the family, make room for every member to partake in problem-solving, encourage connection as they figure out how to greet these changes.

When I sit in a room with a family, I tell myself, I might not have that particular priority had my baby sister not died when I was the right age and personality to take the event so personally, to be so open when it called to my curiosity and compassion. But she did. And I was.

Perhaps everyone has one or two crises that stand out beyond all other times of upheaval because of when they came along or the consequences that followed. Perhaps we're not supposed to fully "get over" these life-forming events but rather to allow their lessons to ripen, and then tease out the lessons and legacy.

The Search for My Elderly Young Girl

Sid, an eighty-seven-year-old client, sat across from me in the afternoon light. He was telling me about his long-dead parents. Suddenly, he said, "How old are you?"

"Almost seventy."

He laughed, clapped his hands. "Why, you're just an elderly young girl!" Big smile. He ran his hands through thick white hair and winked.

His words awakened a sense of falling. What *was* an elderly young girl? If I was one, wouldn't I know what constituted one?

I was well into "growing older." Retired from university teaching, I was winding down my clinical practice as a therapist who worked with elders and their families. Long-divorced, a grandmother of five, I felt nourished by friendships and family connections. A choir, writing group, book club, discussion group, swimming and gardening punctuated my life. How to be a vibrant, engaged senior was the best puzzle I'd ever been handed.

From a young age I was drawn to older people: white hair and relaxed breasts and bellies, spotted hands folded like doves, hummed songs. I wanted to be around them: kindergarten teacher, family housekeeper, everyone's grandparents. Their stories opened worlds of wartime rations, immigration, struggles with friends, corsets and suspenders, romance. Their voices and stories gripped my imagination. They laughed heartily, finished thoughts, expressed interest, thanked me for asking about them.

I couldn't wait to be older. I wanted to be like them, settled inside. I don't recall why I chose fifty, but it was my gateway to the best part of life. My mom, whose favourite age had been seventeen, couldn't understand.

But fifty began what I'd imagined: engaging work, friends, romance. I was healthy, had energy, liked the way I looked. I felt like "me." My children moved in and out but were slowly latching on to their own lives. I counselled seniors in their seventies, eighties, nineties, and their children. They showed me their aging. Stories of both generations filled my heart, challenged my creativity. My clients found it reassuring that I was a mid-life daughter of an old mother who took care of her husband, became widowed. That I had mid-life children of my own was important. Clients wanted to compare experiences. Their parents were living so long! Too few family stories illuminated how to "be old" at 88 or 95 or 103.

"How do ninety-year-olds have a decent life after their friends die?"

"How long *might* my mom live? She's eighty-seven and going strong! How can I do this?"

"Teach me how to be seventy-five — and like it."

Every client wanted to experience a sense of *fit*. I shared with them that those willing to loosen their hold on what was and turn toward what is became more open, relaxed. Many wanted help figuring out how to do this.

Years before, as a university teacher and researcher, I met Ted when I interviewed him, his wife and their adult children about changes related to treatment of serious illness — my then current area of study. Grey-haired, wearing a coat and tie, Ted leaned forward, elbows resting on thighs; his wife sat next to him in loose clothing, no makeup, curly hair pulled back. Four children assured me they wanted to be there. I felt eager and anxious; I'd never had so many family members at an interview.

Weeks before, Ted's wife had undergone surgery and volunteered for my study. For the two years until she died, I interviewed her and her family every six months. No family in my study had been so enthusiastic. After his wife's death, Ted said those conversations were the best he'd ever had; he wanted to continue. Why? Did he want a therapist? A girlfriend?

When we first began to swap ideas over dinner, I was in my early thirties, serious about my career, stretched by divorce and single parenthood. Ted was retired, sixty-one, the same age as my mom. His children weren't much younger than me. Ted and I conversed like peers.

Our connection developed slowly, like a medieval tapestry.

When he asked, "How is a young woman so interested in aging?" I told him about my grandmother's lap, my lifelong desire to be older.

"Ha! You started early! Unusual!"

My research and counselling discoveries dovetailed with Ted's interest in retirees like him. He read, was politically active, worked on projects that benefited seniors. "I'm especially interested in what's known about older men," he said. "And I want to hear how *you* are aging." His eyes twinkled.

For thirty years, Ted and I met several times a year. We didn't socialize outside of our dinners.

Ted would pull index cards covered with notes out of his jacket: housing, women's apparent need for a man, dementia. What did I think? What was I reading? I began to take my own observations and questions to dinner. What was he like when he was my age? What did he think aging would be like? Where did his ideas come from?

"It's one thing when you're well, another when you're not," he offered, then described changes in temperament, family and sense of future as peers became ill and died. "I don't yet know my unwell self, do you?"

"Only in episodes. Crises, but nothing that left me dependent. I learned about living with illness from my dad, and from clients."

"What did they teach you about staying afloat when seriously ill?"

I had to think about how to express that. "To hang on to activities, relationships, anything that evokes meaning, connection and hope. Even a fraction of what was seems to help whoever is vulnerable stay nimble and . . . graceful. Being well *and* sick takes . . . gymnastics."

"Yes. My wife struggled. And *I* struggled — a lot — with that."

Mainly clients wanted to know what I thought about their aging. But Ted and I pooled thoughts about what it takes to be a successful elder. I heard myself talk about *my* aging, illness, end of life. We heard one another's evolving sense of growing older, changing relationships, dreams, ideas about dying and death. He listened, witnessed me as I did him. It was thrilling.

Ted and I were careful to avoid over-emphasizing what was missing — the darker parts of aging. Without being blindly optimistic, we focused on how to emphasize what was still just fine. We explored how feeling balanced seemed essential for enjoyment, especially when ambushed by aging-related changes.

By the time Ted died at ninety-one, I was the age he'd been when we met. We had grown older together.

We had become one another's teacher and pupil.

We had revelled in knowing neither of us had answers.

When I told Mom about dinners with Ted, she asked, of course, if we were romantically involved, then said he was too old for me. I loved her for being consistent: all men (unless "old") were potential husbands. My job was to stay youthful and attractive. Her friends could not think I was too old to marry again.

As Ted and Mom aged, contrasts between them became more marked. This pushed me to focus on her aging and reflect on her and Dad when they were my age. I saw how they shaped my own beliefs: my commitment to exercise and friendship mirrored Mom's; my decision to reinvent myself professionally mirrored my father's mid-life career switch.

While Ted opened himself to aging, Mom pushed it away. Ted shared thoughts and feelings; Mom focused on her fountain of youth — appearance. When she was eighty, during a cocktail party my oldest brother and I, fifty-eight and fifty, watched Mom, radiant in crimson and black evening pants, hair swept back. She glanced at my grey hair, approached us, a forefinger raised. "Do not tell my friends how old you are!" she whispered.

By the time I was ten, I knew I wasn't drawn to Mom's constantly-in-motion competence. She didn't pause. Her energy — she — felt chaotic, but I admired how she cheerfully got seven children up for breakfast, herded us to dinner, talked with household help, fed dogs, hosted parties. When on her fortieth birthday she appeared in a sequined sheath dress, her lips ruby red, I held my breath. *My mom was more beautiful than anyone else's mom.* I knew I would never be so sparkly, spunky.

When I first talked with her about growing older, she described dance cards, debutante balls, trips into New York City on the train. In my teens, she bought me stylish clothes, made sure I attended fraternity weekends at my brothers' universities, but furrowed her brow when I said, "This is *not* the best time of life."

"Don't miss the fun. You'll get old," she admonished. She worried about me a lot.

We were so different. In 1960, when I was fifteen, I longed to jump over frenzied teenage energy and confusing emotions. My focus on schoolwork made Mom's shoulders rise, her voice turn crispy. "It's Friday night. You should be going out." To reassure her, I chatted about friends, wore clothes she bought, but became furtive about learning, reading, writing about questions she couldn't answer. I sneaked out to meet my boyfriend, drank my parents' booze.

Dad worried about me less.

In 1960, when a clot led to an amputation of his left leg, he became a new father. Dad's previous breezy, social self diminished; in its place, a father more reflective, able to listen, share more. He talked about his parents, his youth, asked questions: "Do you think my mom knew how sick she was before she died?" "How does a person decide to give up?"

Mom zeroed in on Dad's appointments and daughters' activities. She worked hard to be cheerful. Determined to maintain a social life despite a now-reluctant husband, she orchestrated small cocktail parties. Dad patted a hassock, invited me to talk when I came in from school. For hours he sat in his wingback chair, smoking, always ready to talk. I was comfortable around a dad like this.

No one knew when the next clot would hit. When it did, scurrying around. Hospitals. Surgeons. And weeks in bed. Dad's hair turned white, his skin loosened, but he got well again. I never thought of him as old, just sick now and again.

"I don't know if I can do this, Crissy," he said as fingers drummed hospital linens. "I still feel the gangrenous leg. But it's not there. What if *it* never goes away? What if I have to live on morphine? How can I be a good husband, father?"

"You'll always be my dad, no matter what."

"It's so hard on your mom."

I didn't know what to do about that.

When his phantom pain stopped, I watched Dad figure out how to be a one-legged professional, parent, social partner. He played piano and jazz saxophone — pleasures from his youth — read, took up ping-pong, drank more. I was warmed when he asked me about my boyfriend, studies. We talked about money, my future. He taught me about being sometimes-sick.

The difference in my parents' perspectives was dazzling.

As a university student I was drawn to courses about human behaviour and self-inquiry. I told Dad about them; he'd studied psychology. He wanted to be the subject of a major essay I wrote on pain. I interviewed him strategically, learned about words like *agony*, *despair*, *hopeless*. He told me he'd wanted to end his life, and why he didn't. His words lived on in me. I felt privileged to hear them.

"Just keep going to school, Crissy, until you don't have to depend on anyone. Carry your life on your back. Everything else works itself out." I didn't know what he meant, but I loved being a student and had no trouble pleasing him. He died days after I finished my master's degree. I was twenty-four years old.

When Mom was in her eighties, she and I sat on her paisley sofa with a ritualistic nightcap. I treasured moments when she turned reflective.

"You're so much like your father."

She sipped her drink, looked at me with a small squint.

"You look so much like him, act like him. So . . . serious! You think about *everything*. It's like having him here."

I saw how much I had drawn on, been drawn by, my father.

At seventy-three, as I now enter my fourth year of episodic illness and wellness, I still explore my Elderly Young Girl. What is clear is my bone-deep need to be my own witness, to figure it out in writing, in remembered conversations with people like Ted and Dad. I see how I learn from elders who teach as they talk, who allow me to witness their aging. Their stories imprint me. Like an archaeologist, I brush away years of sand from emotional fossils; this allows me to see connections between their worlds and mine. In showing me how to go backwards in order to move forward, they turn me into my own teacher.

Illness has sharpened my awareness of when less is more. When friends tell stories about cruises, volcano hikes, cycling or watching the Northern Lights, I see my Elderly Young Girl doesn't have that kind of "bucket list." I don't compare my internal careful life with their adventures. For me, travel involves energy fluctuations, bowel disturbance, risks in being away from health care, need for rest. I don't argue with my body. And I've already had many travel adventures.

Even so, I'm not done yet.

I've been reshaped as I've learned to live with illness. Much of what I did ten years ago continues — meditation, writing, exercise, music, participation in groups, reading, gardening, connecting. But because I can't predict how I will feel, activities happen less often, are shorter and quieter, get cancelled.

Like other aging people, my biorhythms march to their own drummer. With the arrival of pain, I sort out the voice of my aging body from signs I'm becoming sick, pay attention to both. My knowledge of bodies helps me temper dread. I keep my heart tuned to how to fit in my life; I work to be nimble. Activities that were once foreground become background, recede to conserve energy, highlight joy, patience, hope, laughter, intimacy, reflection.

Sometimes I sit in my cherry-red leather wingback chair to watch birds whirl and buzz. Think about Ted and Dad. When I asked my father what he was doing as he sat looking out at his garden, he said, "Just figuring things out, honey." Ted said he watched clouds because they helped his soul catch up with changes in his life.

Mostly, when I watch my birds, I sense I have what I need to face what comes along. As long as I take time to be with whatever is new, name it, remind myself how well I've been taught, I figure it out. It's what I do.

Notes on Music

Age 6, 1951
The music room is always cold in winter. Dad and I both wear sweaters. He warms up my hands as we sit down on the piano bench. It is my first year of piano lessons with Mrs. Bostelmann. I want to please my father. He wants all of his six children to play piano. He does. Mom does. It's what children are supposed to do, especially children of a talented musician.

Age 73, 2018
At 9:00 a.m. on Sundays I turn on CBC Choral Concert and return to my red chair with another cup of coffee. I don't remember when I began this ritual, but it's so familiar and engrained I miss it when I am away from home on a Sunday. I close my eyes and allow myself to be swept away by whatever group is singing.

Age 55, 2000

Pat Metheny's guitar music flows under the door of Lee's office and into the hall. I stand outside the door and listen before I knock. Lee and I just met three days ago, and I know almost nothing about him except what I learned at the think tank on creativity we both attended at UBC. "Do you like Metheny?" he asks when he opens the door. My desire to be touched has already been launched by the music.

Age 17, 1962

Last night Dad and I went to two jazz performances on the beach. Tonight musicians arrived for a jam session, Dad on tenor saxophone, someone named Bud on piano, a drummer, a clarinet player, and the saxophone player who stared at me last night. Johnny. I stand next to the piano, watch and listen. I feel proud to know every tune. The men place lit cigarettes in an ashtray on top of the piano while they play.

Age 5, 1950

Late at night my mom gets my older sister Nancy and me out of bed, awakens us. Party guests are downstairs. Dad has taught us two-part harmony to "Tell Me Why," my mom's favourite song, and she wants her friends to hear us sing. In our flannel nighties we stumble down the back stairs. The dining room table is covered with wine glasses. Sis and I sing. Everyone claps. We climb the stairs and get back into bed, pleased with ourselves.

Age 7, 1952

Nearby, in Mrs. Bostelmann's living room, sits my sister Nancy, one year older. She has a piano lesson after mine. I already know I'll never catch up to Nancy, no matter how hard I practise. Mrs. Bostelmann stands behind me, leans over to guide my fingers, her large breasts on my shoulders, touching my ears. She is talking, I know, about Wagner, Beethoven. Nancy and I will play a duet at the next recital. I am filled with dread.

Age 7, 1952
My oldest brother Chip, fourteen, has a new radio, brown, wood, a huge circular dial. He has labelled all the stations he can get, tells me about the radio stations in New York. While he types away at a neighbourhood newspaper he produces, I lie on the floor of his room with my ear to the speaker, transfixed by the musical stories pouring out of this magic box.

Age 20, 1965
On a boat in Copenhagen, Joanne, a fellow traveller I recently met, begins to sing American folk songs with a guitar she carries everywhere. I join in, harmonizing. Soon, passengers on the boat are singing, smiling, clapping. That evening Joanne suggests we play guitar and sing in a tiled bathroom in the small hotel where we are staying. "The echo will make us sound great," she says. Then, "Here, I'll teach you a few chords." I am thrilled.

Age 15, 1960
My high school has hired a man named Ron, not much older than the students, to create a choral department. He hand-picks members of the first choir, not because they are musical but because they are enthusiastic about creating something brand new. I am thrilled when he picks me. I become an alto. For three years I sing with this same group of peers. We win the state championship more than once.

Age 37, 1982

About two dozen guests from around the world sit and stand around the campfire at the Flying U Ranch in BC's Cariboo country. I am there to horseback-ride with my sons, ten and twelve years old. I get my guitar from our cabin, join the campfire group and begin to sing folk songs. My children watch from ten feet away, ready to be embarrassed, but move closer, eyes wide. Guests sing along, some in their own languages.

Age 4, 1949

My four older siblings are at school and I am home alone with my mom, a rarity. I follow her from room to room while she tidies up. She sings and taps the bottom of the metal wastepaper baskets. I recognize the songs from the radio. Her words are like those words, her sounds like those sounds. I try to sing along.

Age 11, 1956

My father is plunking away at the piano, talking to himself. Since his heart attack, he has taken piano lessons, even though he knows how to play. I lie on my bed in my bedroom, about ten feet from the piano, hear him work at chords I do not recognize from my own piano lessons a few years ago. He plays one chord over and over. I know he is training his fingers.

Age 20, 1965

After I return from Europe I date a law student who plays guitar, who teaches me what he knows about chords and picking. He has nimble fingers and a voice that wanders off key, so when we go to parties, he plays and I sing. Fifty years later, because he married my college roommate, Steve and I will still know one another, get together to play and sing. When I say to him, "I don't think I was a very good guitar player back then, was I?" he will guffaw, "You were terrible. But you could sing."

Age 57, 2002

For weeks my three sisters and I sing a cappella to our mom, who is slowly dying. We sing her favourite song, "Tell Me Why," and our favourite, "May You Always." I am to carry the melody, the easiest part. Four times out of five I miss the same phrase at the end of the tune when it leaves familiar territory. My sisters look at me with patient eyes. I'll never be able to do what they do so easily.

Age 8, 1953

On Christmas Eve, Mom, Dad and my four older siblings and I go to Sand Beach Church to hear my mom sing in the choir. She wears a long blue gown and stands in the middle of a group of men and women, some of whom I know. The church is lit by candles. The youngest children take gifts to the altar. When my mom sings, I feel like I'm going to cry but can't understand why.

Age 11, 1956

My sister Nancy and I practise "You Belong to Me" by Patience and Prudence. It is a hit song on the teen radio list and our voices blend perfectly. We sing it every chance we get to whoever will listen. Singing together is the only real way we could get along with one another at that time.

Age 18, 1963

To cope with the homesickness that plagues me during my first year at university, I sing along with the LP albums

I brought with me. And cry. When my English teacher mentions I look sad, asks what activities I did in high school that brought me joy, I say, "Sing." He invites me to join his church choir. I weep during my first rehearsal but sing twice a week for the remainder of my freshman year.

Age 65, 2010
After taking two SFU Continuing Studies courses on the history of jazz, I write the teacher, Neil Ritchie, tell him I took his course to find that part of my father, who died before I could ask him about his music. I tell him his teaching helped me figure out my father's fascination with jazz, why he chose tenor saxophone, why he collected the artists he did. Neil answers my letter, tells me about music and his father.

Age 57, 2002
During the long humid summer days of my mom's dying, to calm my restlessness, I play CDs of sacred music and lie on my bed, eyes closed, and listen to my younger sister Casey play her cello in the living room. I let the sounds wind around me, pull me away, toss me into a simple peaceful sphere suffused with hope.

Age 16, 1961
On the table next to my bed is a white shoebox-size plastic radio. The circular dial is tuned to 560, WQAM out of Miami. Every afternoon and evening, the week's top ten songs are played. I memorize lyrics, find in the words expression for feelings that otherwise roam restlessly inside me. Sometimes I call the station, dedicate a song to a boy I have a crush on.

Age 18, 1963
The group of friends around me at the poolside party in Fort Lauderdale all like to sing. Many of us are in our high school's chorus. My boyfriend, who I think I want to marry, plays guitar and sings tenor. He looks and sounds like Nick from the Kingston Trio. I harmonize with him when he plays "Chilly Winds."

Age 45, 1990
My friend Paula and I sing in Peter Dent's "Jazz etc." chorus. He selects me for two solos in the next concert. I refuse. "I'll coach you," he says. My nightmare: starting on the wrong note. Which happens, in front of 150 people. I stop, tell the audience, "One of us is on the wrong note," and Peter raises his hand. In the front row a white-haired older woman whispers loudly, "You go, girl!"

Age 63, 2008
My grandchildren Ella, six, and Alexander, five, aren't so sure they want to "go to the theatre with DeeDee" but want to please me, so they agree. On a dark, wet December night I excitedly drive them to Richmond to see *The Sound of Music*. Within the next few days we watch videos of Mary Martin in *Peter Pan* and Betty Hutton in *Annie Get Your Gun*. They mimic "Anything You Can Do (I Can Do Better)," laugh.

Age 68, 2013
I tell myself if I take guitar lessons for a year, I will buy myself a new instrument. At Long and McQuade I meet my first teacher, a mop-haired twenty-something man who laughs a lot. He tells me he taught his eighty-year-old

grandfather to play guitar. After a month of lessons I know he's seriously stoned all the time, thank him for igniting my curiosity, tell him I need a teacher who's a bit closer to my age. He says, "Whatever," and hugs me. My son finds me a new teacher who is perfect.

Age 33, 1978

New to Vancouver, I miss singing, tell myself I should be able to sing barbershop like my dad and older sister, and audition for the Lions Gate chapter of the Sweet Adelines chorus. For a year I happily sing bass, work hard to remember all I once knew about reading music. I join a quartet and we rehearse madly in hopes we will place at the regional competition. We do. Honourable mention. I announce this to my mom and sisters right away.

Age 24, 1969

When my husband and I go to Europe for several months, I don't take my guitar. I will buy a new one when we get to Spain. Although my husband doesn't sing or play a musical instrument, he is an enthusiastic listener and always enjoys my singing. In a shop in Barcelona I pick out a new guitar, watch while it is tuned, take delight in getting to know this new friend.

Age 50, 1995

My younger sister Suzie, forty-three, invites me to her class-room, where she teaches music basics to inner-city kids, most of them from Haiti, El Salvador. A chorus of different languages. Across the school patio, a sign reads *Welcome, Miss Criss.* The children sing Canadian music, play percussion on a sculpture of dump metal they created in the school courtyard. I watch my sister, a maestro. In awe.

Age 10, 1956

Church hymns being played on the piano. Mom doesn't know I am behind the closed door to my room. She has told me often she only plays piano when she knows no one is home. Her voice rings clear, moves easily through one Christmas carol, then another. "Angels we have heard on high . . . Glor-or-i-a, Glor-or-i-a." I hum along. Smile. Don't move.

Age 53, 1998

My class in family dynamics at UBC has eighty students; many are immigrants. I introduce the class by playing music, lyrics on an overhead. I link content about the music and today's lecture. Initially students retreat into silence. When I ask them to bring in music with meaning to them, to present it to the class along with the singer or composer's family dynamics, they jump at the chance.

Age 8, 1953

Music from downstairs. Aunt Margaret's laughter above the jazzy song she is playing on the piano. Nancy and I lie on the floor at the top of the wide stairs leading to the living room. I can watch through the banisters. A clutch of my parents' friends and siblings surround Margaret, arms around one another. My aunt Carol's voice rises above the rest. Recently she told me she had studied opera.

Age 9, 1954

My father has switched Nancy and me to a new piano teacher. Mr. Cappiello teaches chords, popular music, not classical. Nancy waits in the next room while I have my lesson. Mr. Cappiello slides his hand up under my dress, his fingers inside my underpants. I start to wear heavy snow pants even when there's no snow. I quit piano. Dad asks why. I shrug.

Age 40, 1985

Sam, my new piano teacher, comes to my house. I have a piano, want to play, even though I don't care if I'm ever very good. He's a gentle man. I tell him he cannot sit on the piano bench with me, no matter what. He doesn't. After the fourth lesson he tells me he's not equipped to deal with the intensity of my anxiety and doesn't understand why I get so nervous. Neither do I. I quit piano lessons, again.

Age 50, 1995

A man I am crazy about sends me CDs of music. He is a man of few words, which draws me to listen to every word of lyrics for clues about his feelings. The songs are about love, waiting, yearning. I play the music for my son's girlfriend, ask her to help me interpret the words, confirm what I am hoping is serious interest in me. She says, "Maybe."

Age 73, 2018

Since my sister Suzie sent me a music stand to encourage my guitar-playing, I play four to five times a week. I move the stand from room to room, settle on the living room, in front of the window where I can see my garden. No matter how clumsy my old fingers are, I feel lighter and refreshed after doing scales, practising picking, singing old favourites. Some days I think I'm improving.

Age 8, 1953

Nancy, Mom and I are in the car driving across upstate New York to Melody Circus, a summer Broadway festival that takes place under a tent. "One day I will take you to Broadway. For now, this will do," Mom tells us. The seats go fully round the stage, where we see *Carousel* and *Oklahoma*. Nancy and I lean forward, slurping up every sound, word, colour of costume.

Age 43, 1988

I meet my older sister Nancy in Seattle. We are going to hear Marion McPartland, a jazz pianist and friend of our father's. Marion has reserved seats, joins us after the show. We reminisce about jam sessions at Dad and Mom's. Nancy grins as she describes playing duets with Marion. In the elevator I ask Marion if she and Dad were lovers. "That's for me to know and you to always wonder about," she says with a smile.

Age 24, 1969

My father is dead and we are sorting through his things. All of his seven children and his wife want some piece of his musical history. I open his binders of sheets of jazz tunes. His small tidy writing reveals lyrics, composer and arranger, lists of songs played by him and other once-upon-a-time members of his band from Princeton during a recent reunion. We all know Dad's binders belong to Nancy. I take a black-and-white photo of him in a tux leading his big band.

Age 70, 2016

Drugged and silent, I lie in a bed in the downstairs apartment of my own house, too weak from surgery to climb stairs. I have cancer. Chunks of my body have been removed and my younger sister Casey is here to take care of me. She rents a cello, sits nearby, gentle as a breath, playing music that swirls in my sloshy brain and takes me to a place of hope.

Age 24, 1969

In front of the fireplace are my older brothers Metty and Chip and their wives, my sister Nancy, my husband and me. After we tune our guitars, we pass a joint around, sing songs we all know by heart. Dad's tunes from the thirties, Mom's Broadway songs, four-part harmonics from the fifties, Kingston Trio, John Denver. We think we sound great.

Age 16, 1961

With no radio in his VW Bug, my twenty-one-year-old brother Bart and I sing as we travel from Fort Lauderdale to New Orleans, where he is attending university. Mom has sent me along "as company" on this trip. A couple of years ago he introduced me to Jimmy Rogers's and Buddy Holly's music, so we work on "Kisses Sweeter Than Wine" and "Everyday." We have never sung duets before, but our voices blend well.

Age 4, 1949

My grandmother and mom sing the same lullaby: "Strawberries, strawberries, flaxen hair just like gold. And everyone said, her lips were as red as the strawberries she sold." At bedtime, I ask to hear it over and over, until I can sing it through with no help. Mom tells me I am her strawberry baby, born in June.

Age 25, 1970

The new friends my husband and I make when we move to Texas like to make music. In the group are a pianist, bass player, saxophonist, drummer, guitar player. "Any chance you sing?" asks Ron, the pianist. "We need a singer." My secret dreams of being the girl singer for a big band push forth when I say, "Sort of." For a few years, in the confines of Ron's living room, I hold a mike, close my eyes and happily imagine I am just that girl.

Age 53, 1998
Drawn like a moth to a flame, I join Vancouver's Bursting with Broadway chorus, where I sing Broadway showtunes. Thrilled to be part of this large group, to be led by Dominique Hogan, the director, I sing my heart out. Her enthusiasm and respectful encouragement remind me of my high school choral director. I tell her I am singing because of him.

Age 70, 2015
Before I meet up with a group of friends I have seen every other year for over fifty years, I send music to everyone, tell them we need to enjoy one another musically again. Everyone agrees to practise whatever instrument they play, polish up "Four Strong Winds," "Don't Think Twice," "Nancy Whiskey," tunes in G or C. Our still-okay voices make up for our hesitant fingers. With no missed notes, we sing "May the Lord Bless You and Keep You," a standard for our high school chorus.

Part Two

The Change

When I was forty-six my mom started to worry about my sanity. I had mentioned to her that I was menopausal and this exposed in her a worry that wormed its way into conversations as often as she could manage it. She honestly believed, I discovered, that "the change" (as she called menopause) made women go crazy. Even greater than her worry about me was her concern about my older sister Nancy's mental health. We were both menopausal at the same time.

"So what is it about menopause, Mom?" I asked one spring when Nancy and I visited her at her home in South Carolina. I had flown east from Vancouver, where I lived with my two young adult sons; my older sister had driven north from Florida, where she lived with her husband. We met at Mom's annually and looked forward to it. Sometimes our two younger sisters joined us, but that year, Mom's seventy-sixth, it was just us two oldest daughters.

When this conversation happened, we were sitting in her living room sipping Scotch. We'd had dinner with her and her husband, our stepfather, who now watched TV in the bedroom. One of Mom's favourite rituals was a nightcap before bed. Over the years we'd learned she sometimes opened up when she sat on the paisley sofa sipping Scotch; she became more personal than usual.

"You act like Nancy and I will become serial killers just because we've stopped bleeding. I don't even remember your menopause. What happened?" I sought her eyes. Maybe I'd get lucky.

"Nothing," she tossed back. She took a sip of her Scotch and set the glass carefully in front of her. Her eyes looked down at the coffee table.

"What about your sisters? Your mom? Tell me about them."

I exchanged glances with Nancy, who sat next to Mom, her eyes trained on Mom's profile.

"Well, Mom didn't do very well." A pause. "She just had a hard time." Her eyes met mine, turned toward Nancy's.

For the next hour my sister and I teased out of Mom what "a hard time" meant. What she told us rearranged everything we thought we knew about our grandmother. Because Mom avoided stories about anything that was dark or disturbing, this was an unusual, potent occasion.

She told us that in the mid-1930s, when she was eighteen years old, she'd completed boarding school in Philadelphia and was living in Manhattan. There, as did other wealthy young women, she attended a finishing school and lived at the Barbizon Hotel. Daily she went to class to learn how to set a proper table, open a conversation with a guest, arrange flowers for the foyer, dress for dinner, sit, walk, shake hands. In other words, she was in training to become a wife who knew how to "run a home." On weekends she and my father, a senior at Princeton University and a jazz saxophone player, frequented New York's jazz bars and went to the theatre. Life glittered.

I knew my mom had been a stunning young woman and could easily imagine her gliding down red-carpeted halls of the Barbizon Hotel, climbing into a cab on Fifth Avenue, my handsome father holding her elbow. Pictures of her at that time reveal a tall, slender, athletic woman, dressed in slim skirts and jaunty hats. A broad confident smile and a frisky, flirtatious look reach out from black-and-white photos. The images exude an air of privilege. It's never been surprising to me that my father wanted to know who she was when he first saw her on a dance floor.

"Twice," said Mom to my sister and me, "during the time I lived at the Barbizon, Mom visited me." My grandmother was then in her mid-forties, my age. "She'd called to say she needed to get away for a few days, arrived on the afternoon train. She was unsteady on her feet, crying, even talked about killing herself. Her breath smelled of alcohol." She stared at her lap, her hand over her mouth. "I didn't know what to do."

Nancy and I locked eyes. "What happened?"

"She cut herself. Blood. Mentioned a gun. During the second visit she walked to the window, threw it open, threatened to jump."

My sister's face blanched. Her mouth opened. "Oh my heavens! What did you do?"

"I grabbed her by the back of her dress. It was awful, just awful." Mom's head wagged back and forth. Her thumbs worried with one another. She took a long drink of Scotch.

"I had no idea she was . . . so unhappy. She'd never been before."

I imagined Mom, still a teenager, exposed to her mother's underbelly. I reached over and grabbed her hand.

Mom's mother was the most refined, socially elegant person I've ever met. A woman of enormous confidence, she laughed readily and loved life. Her voice, musical and elastic, was mesmerizing. Time with her was magical: music, theatre, laughter, new experiences. She loved surprises and knew exactly how to create them. To be with this grandmother was to feel like the only person on her planet. What Mom was saying flew around inside me like a frightened bird.

"What did she talk about, Mom?"

"Was she . . . crazy?" My sister said the word *crazy* as if it could unleash a noxious gas into the room.

Mom leaned forward. "She said awful things. About Dad. And her mother, too — and she barely knew her mother! She didn't make any sense. She went nuts." Another long sip of Scotch. "That's all. It happens. It's the change." Her voice went soft. "I just didn't know what to do." Pleading, her eyes sought mine, Nancy's.

Mom told us over and over how terrified she'd been. "During Mom's second visit, I called your dad to help me figure out what to do with her. She was drunk, hysterical." Dad was twenty-three years old.

"Your father didn't yet know Mom and Dad very well; they'd only met once. He did what he thought was right, didn't know how wrong it was to call an ambulance, have Mom taken where people went when they . . . He didn't know how outrageous it would be for Mom to be admitted to a public institution for psychiatric patients."

Her mother was taken where other emotionally disturbed New Yorkers were taken, a place called "the snake pit," where she waited for two days until her husband arranged for her release.

I now understood a comment Mom's sister had made a few years before, when she said it took several years for my father to be forgiven for an "unfortunate decision" he'd made before he married into the family.

When Mom finished talking, all three of us became silent. Our breathing was shallow, as if air had been sucked from the room.

"It only lasted a year. Her craziness," Mom said suddenly.

My eyes widened. "A *year*? And then it just stopped?"

"Yes, thankfully, it just disappeared. And there was Mom again. The mom I knew." She smiled at us.

As we talked about what a relief it had been when my grandmother "bounced back," I wondered what clicked her craziness into motion, and what clicked it off again. I knew her menopause had lasted longer than a year.

I wondered about other experiences in my then forty-six-year-old grandmother's life. Suddenly I remembered something else Mom's sister had said as I sat with her in her sun room, asking her about her mother and her grandmother. I'd asked why there were so few stories about her grandmother.

"I never met my grandmother. She died young."

"How young?"

"When she was forty-six. Mom was just a girl, a teenager. I don't even know how she died. But imagine what it was like for Mom and her sisters! No mom to take care of them."

Forty-six years old. That was the same age *my* frantic grandmother was when she got on the train and fled to New York, knocked on Mom's door and said things an eighteen-year-old had no way of understanding.

I told Mom about my conversation with her sister, said I was sure this death left in its wake a house full of distraught children, one of whom was Mom's mother.

"Maybe your mom's horrible upset was related to that devastating event in her childhood, Mom. Maybe it came back to her, made her remember. As a child she would have been too young to make sense of so much loss. When she got to the same age her mom was when she died, maybe her grief unleashed. It's called an 'anniversary reaction.' "

Mom looked at me as if I'd gone nuts. Her lips pushed into a pout. "Don't be ridiculous," she said stubbornly. "Some women just fall apart for a while. Mom was one of them. And maybe *her* mom was, too. The change is like that. And that's *that*." Her eyes were dark. She tipped the last of her Scotch into her mouth and stood up. Nancy and I did, too.

As Nancy took empty glasses to the kitchen, Mom leaned toward my ear. "Watch out for your sister, she's a lot like Mom."

Hurricane Days

The ring of the phone at 6:00 a.m. catapulted me from sleep into a pit of dread; I drew a deep breath, offered a raspy "Hello?"

My older sister Nancy's voice pounced. "Hurricane Floyd is headed toward the southeast — South Carolina, Georgia and northern Florida — and it will be a Category 5 storm by tonight." A breath. "It's going to blow right through Mother's picture window. We have to *do* something."

Like many who watch a lot of weather news, she plunged into details of wind speed, location and time of landfall, and expected precipitation, her voice strung tight. "It will be the biggest storm to ever hit the United States. A state of emergency has *already* been declared, even though it won't hit land for hours." She released a chest full of air. "Mother and you-know-who are refusing to leave their house. I just got off the phone with them." Silence. I was supposed to say something intelligent.

"I need to make coffee so I can think," I managed. "It's six o'clock in the morning."

"Oh God, I forgot. East Coast–West Coast, of course. I'm really sorry. Go make coffee, call me after your second cup. I'll be here boarding up. This is wild." Click.

I pushed myself into a sitting position, stared at the wall for a moment, then went downstairs to grind coffee beans.

That year, 1999, my youngest sister, oldest brother and sister Nancy all lived on Florida's east coast, more than five hours south of Mother. My other three siblings and I were scattered elsewhere. I was the lone sibling on the West Coast.

Mother and her husband left Florida in their sixties to live in South Carolina. They chose a location without thinking about how their children would get to them when they got old and needed attention from us. They chose the lowland coast, rich with rivers and wetlands, the Atlantic just out beyond islands that dot the shore waters. To get to them was a geographic obstacle course of two-lane roads through swamps.

By 8:30 a.m. I had talked with four siblings and Mother and had cancelled classes and clients to be on duty for what was spiralling into a family emergency. I put on jeans, made another pot of coffee and put a notepad on the kitchen counter near the phone.

All seven of us children, I learned, were agitated by the worrisome weather and our mother's refusal to leave her house. To soothe ourselves, we analyzed the house and its capacity to withstand wind and the twenty-six-foot tides that were anticipated. They would cross the low road in front of Mother's property and drown her two-story, ground-level, no-basement house on a bay. The offshore islands might buffer, but they would be no match for the fury of Floyd. My oldest brother Chip said the 150-mile-per-hour winds would surely rip off their old, mouldy roof.

In two-person conversations, we perseverated. What would it take to get them out of the house? Our ideas became ridiculous. Every few minutes, a call detailed the most recent conversation with resolute Mother. Her message was clear: she and our stepfather would stay put.

Hundreds of miles away from any child, she had us cornered.

A late-morning phone call from Chip revealed he'd learned two hospitals down the road from Mother had been evacuated. He was furious.

"I don't understand why they are being so . . . stupid," he sputtered. "Don't they see they will *drown*? *Die*?"

I knew he hoped I could do something powerful enough to make them leave their home. But I knew from my lifetime of experience that I had no more magical power over her than he did. Once Mother's heels were dug in, she was a force to reckon with.

While my brother worried into my right ear, I imagined eighty-five-year-old Mother answering the phone every few minutes in her kitchen, wearing her little navy blue stretch pants and yellow golf shirt. She'd be perched on one of the stools by the butcher-block island, staring out the window at her garden, in exquisite bloom. Her phone must have rung thirty times this morning; she would love that. I saw her smiling every time a phone call tumbled into her kitchen as *all* her children and probably a couple of her husband's checked in, worried, fretted noisily. Her centrality in everyone's life, confirmed, would leave her high, feeling important. This kind of activity was much more invigorating than being cloistered in her too-tight world, caring for her eighty-seven-year-old husband with Alzheimer's.

"What did she say to you when you talked to her just now?" I asked my brother.

His voice turned falsetto: "We'll be *fine*, dear, don't worry so much about us. We're just two old people. We'll go upstairs with the dogs if the water rises. I've already packed picnic baskets with dog food and a few things for us. We'll have everything we need. If we blow away, well, I guess we blow away." He coughed.

"Jesus," I said to him, "this is awful. I hate this. I don't know what to do. You know Mother when she gets a hair up her ass. If she says they won't leave, you *know* what that means."

He continued, "She told me the church called yesterday and offered them a ride; they were trying to make sure all the old folks in the congregation had transportation out of town. *And* she said her friend Beatrice was willing to take them and all five of those dogs in her car." My brother didn't need to tell me Mother had turned down both offers. "I'm done with this now," he said. "I have to worry about my own house. Goodbye." Click.

A familiar leaden cape of worry settled around my shoulders, a feeling I got when others expected me to unknot a difficult family puzzle. As I put the receiver down, I realized I wanted to stop answering the phone. Hide. Take off. Not think about any of it. *I don't even live on the frigging East Coast. Why should I have anything to do with this? Let them handle it. I handle enough.*

By early afternoon, Casey and Nancy had hatched a plan. Casey would drive five hours from Atlanta to Mother's, scoop her, her husband and their dogs up and drive back to Atlanta. There, they would hole up in a pet-friendly Holiday Inn until the storm was over.

"I will just arrive at their house," said Casey emphatically. "No notice. Walk in the front door and tell them that they will be mad at me for ten years, but I can take it — just get the dogs, pyjamas, toothpaste and whatever else and get *in* the damned car!" She sounded frantic but proud. "I'm leaving in an hour." Click. I imagined her pulling up in Mother's driveway in her tie-dyed T-shirt and shorts, carrot-coloured hair bristling.

A continent away, I flicked on the TV. Hurricane Floyd from space. The storm covered the entire American Southeast and Caribbean like a circus tent. I knew my siblings were putting shutters on windows and pulling lawn furniture into garages. I'd spent the 1960s in South Florida; I knew how hurricanes stripped away all sense of safety. Wind and water went wherever they damn well wanted to, until they didn't want to anymore. Beaches washed into hotel lobbies, main streets became rivers, lawns were denuded.

Mother. She too had been there during the hurricanes in the 1960s. During one, all our bushes and trees were swept down our street. She knew what it took to protect a house from rain and wind. I'd seen her hustle patio furniture inside, lug potted plants up close to the house. I'd sat with her while she listened to the wind roar and worried about what was happening outside shutter-covered windows. Why wasn't she afraid *now*?

I thought about Casey cruising along the Interstate, then manoeuvring narrow roads, crossing dozens of bridges, and snaking her way through the lowlands as winds increased, her car swaying, pushed around like a Tinkertoy. A fine sweat broke out on my forehead.

A few minutes later, Casey, her voice staccato: The trip was off. Savannah had been evacuated and all roads leading to it from the south were closed. Traffic now headed only west and north, away from the storm. "Turn on the news. Even Canada will have aerial pictures of the highways. It's bumper to bumper for miles and miles. Entire cities are on the move, headed west. People are really freaked out." I turned on the weather channel. Lines of cars inched away from the threat of huge tides. Just looking at it made me feel claustrophobic.

"You're right. Christ, where's everyone going?"

"To emergency shelters. Churches. Schools. Public are-nas. *Anywhere* but near the ocean. Okay, gotta go." Click.

I dialled Mother's number. She picked it up on the first ring, singing a cheery "Hello?"

"Hi, Mother, it's me again. How are things going now?" I forced a casual voice.

"Oh, I'm glad you called. I have exciting news! The *National Guard* came to the house just now — the nicest young man! He told us we *have* to leave. The *president* has declared a *state of emergency*." I imagined her opening her front door to a man in uniform addressing her by name using an official-sounding voice. Oh, how she would love that — she'd always been drawn to men in uniform. I knew her husband would be behind her, his tall gaunt body leaning toward the front door, eyes peering through thick lenses. He would have snapped-to with a salute.

"So they *insisted* you leave?" I gripped the counter to stay calm. By now the winds were getting serious. This wasn't funny *at all*. I felt pissed off. "What will happen now?"

"Oh, we'll go to a shelter." Her voice was a bit dreamy, as if she were planning a day at the beach.

"A shelter? Who will drive? Your husband can't drive in this, his brain doesn't work any more, and you can't *see* very well, Mother. Remember? You have macular degeneration." I had to pinch myself to keep from shouting, *Why didn't you go with Beatrice when she offered?*

"We'll be okay, honey, don't worry about us. Everyone's so *worried* about us. I've never known your brothers to be so *worried*. We're going to be *fine, just fine.*" There was a lilt in her voice. Then hurriedly, as if she remembered what this was all about, she said, "I have to pack now. Goodbye." Click.

After that, no one heard from Mother or her husband for three days.

My siblings and I called one another, detailed the amount of damage the storm had done to the East Coast, worried. "Have you heard from her? No? Okay." Click.

By the end of day two the calls had slowed. We knew the storm hadn't offered the anticipated over-the-top punch. And it hadn't hit Mother's community squarely. The damage was less than expected.

I settled into a soggy concern for my mother's well-being.

For the first time in my life I kept the TV on the weather channel, as if it could assure me I would hear from my mother again. I felt slightly reassured that my business card was in Mother's wallet, red letters scrawled across the top: *Call me if anything happens to my mother.* I knew if something dreadful happened, someone would call me, ask, "Are you Clarissa Green?"

On the afternoon of the second day, Nancy called. "God, how is she doing it?"

"What?"

"You *know* his driving. We both *know* that Mother must be strung tighter than a guy-wire. Being in the passenger seat is true torture. I can just *see* her, shoulders tucked up around her eyes, teeth clenched, praying. God, I should have told her to at least get in the back seat and put on an eye mask."

I thought about old parents I'd met or heard described by mid-life children who came to me for counselling, old parents living on their own when others thought they shouldn't anymore. "They have the right to live at risk" was a sentence I said often. I tried to help mid-life children see that just because *they* were worried didn't mean their parents had to live a careful, sequestered life.

Most mid-life children don't know how, I remembered, to worry about their parents. Most haven't considered that parents do have the *right* to live on their own edge, and may do this quite well. Instead they focus on themselves and their desire to make the worry go away. "If they fall, the consequences of that end up in our laps," they say, "and *I'll* have to pick up the pieces!"

"Do you want the right to live at risk when you are eighty-five?" I ask.

To a one, they have quickly said yes. In the silence following that yes, they become ready themselves to discuss the delicate dance between children and old parents, of respecting risks, independence, worry and trust.

During the hurricane days, I hated the worrying as much as any mid-life child does.

Where the hell was my mother?

Mother eventually called on the evening of the third day. She was more spunky and animated than she'd been in years. The storm had settled down, and everyone who'd been evacuated from eastern South Carolina had been told to go home.

"We're home, dear, all safe and sound. And the dogs are so happy. They're racing around the house like madmen."

A number of her shrubs and a few small trees, she said, were gone, but the house hadn't taken in any water. Her husband was crabby, but she assured me he'd be okay by tomorrow. "He won't remember anything that happened, you know. He's already asking me if we went to a movie about a disaster this afternoon. It's too bad he'll forget the whole thing. We had a marvellous time!" She couldn't wait to have a hot bath and a vodka martini.

Over the next few days, as I asked her about the trip, stories tumbled out about driving for hours and hours — first my stepfather and then Mother behind the wheel — cars packed tightly in long lines, headlights on, everyone headed to shelters in northwest South Carolina.

"There were state troopers," she said, "the *nicest* young men, the *best* manners, and they told us which road to take. We passed *three* shelters before we found one that had room for us." Her voice was buoyant.

"Their" shelter had been a huge gymnasium filled with cots, long tables loaded with soup and sandwiches, children and parents, old folks, rich and poor, all colours, milling around.

"It was just like the United Nations!" she exclaimed.

A nearby football field, turned muddy by the driving rain, was filled with parked cars. Their car was on the far side, well away from the gymnasium.

"In our shelter, everybody had their own little cot, blanket and even a pillow. Your stepfather said it looked like army barracks. In fact, he thought he *was* back in the army. He found some other older men who had been in the service and they gabbed away about the war — you know how he loved that. And the loveliest woman served us soup — homemade, of course — a woman from the local church. We talked about children — she has four — and she raises poodles. I told her about raising cockers in the 1940s." A pause, then: "My heavens, that soup was good."

I couldn't believe what I was hearing. My blind mother and cognitively impaired stepfather had somehow successfully driven hundreds of miles inland and spent several days in a public shelter. Traipsed through mud with dogs on leashes. And they'd had a great time.

"How did the dogs do?"

"I didn't want the dogs to get too nervous, so we stayed with them in the car at night."

"In the car? You *slept* in the car? What about the wind and the rain? The weather was crazy, really crazy!"

"Yes, it was. But we couldn't leave our dogs! We just put the front seats back as far as they could go. My husband got into his pyjamas and I got in my nightie—"

"You *what*?"

"Got in my nightie. I just changed my clothes in the front seat. Then we had a little cocktail and went to sleep. You know the dogs, though; they had to go out in the night. So I put on my white bathrobe, put each dog on a leash and got the umbrella out. My heavens, the wind and rain were so strong I could barely push the door open. But the dogs jumped right out and did their business, right by the car. Just as they finished the umbrella blew inside out. I just let it go up into the sky. I was afraid if I held on we'd *all* go straight up — *whoosh*! — along with the umbrella, just like Mary Poppins." Then she started to laugh. I had to join her.

"All of us got terribly wet. And muddy, of course. I wish I'd packed another nightie. And some towels — the dogs shook all over everything. They didn't much like being out in that storm!" Then she began to laugh again.

"Mother, how did the two of you drive? How did you know where you were going?"

"Oh, we had no idea where we were or where we were going. But I don't think anyone did. Everyone had their lights on, so there were tail lights in front of us and headlights behind. I just followed the two red lights in front. I could see *them* well enough."

Over the next week, Mother talked enthusiastically to all her children. With every phone call, a new tidbit about their adventure emerged: what it was like to squat and pee in a parking lot, how she reassured a frightened child who couldn't find her parents, how she rushed through wind and rain for sandwiches at 9:00 p.m.

My mother, a cog in life's wheel of fortune.

Lost and Found

My stepfather is puzzled by the big house he's lived in for decades with my mother: walls crammed with family pictures, the living room where they have sat with family and friends, how the sliding door to the patio works. He moves ghost-like in the halls, wondering why he left one room for another, stands in the kitchen staring at a wrench, bottle of glue, dog collar in his hand. He hunches over his desk strewn with papers, slides an index finger and eyes down a column of figures, then down the same column of figures again. And again. "Goddamn it!" He pounds the desk, starts again, swears again.

His being lost has been going on for several years. And wherever he has gone, he has not taken Mother with him. In his world, when he talks about it, there is no future. His days are spent in a long-ago time where he draws deeply from a well of experiences that have nothing to do with my mother. Images and remembered conversations flow into him without permission or pause. My mother and their here-and-now life exist only for moments.

When he is absorbed in his years spent in World War II, life with him becomes a curious play. In some scenes, he's on board the carrier he knew well during the war years, or he's on leave with his wife and children. He tells me, as if it happened last week, how he returned from the war alive and his wife died soon after. I can tell from his eyes, animation, and voice tone that he's not here, but in 1945.

His war scenes often go in a loop, when he repeatedly describes, for example, the day he returned from the Pacific. His eyes glaze, as if he's back there on the carrier. With each iteration, his words come more slowly, as if he's overlooked something and will find it if he speaks more carefully.

There are two small pictures on his desk, one of my mother, the other of his first wife, the mother of his children.

"My glue," he says of the striking young woman who stares directly into the lens of the camera, a pouty grin on her face. "My glue," he says again, this time putting his fingertip on Mother's face. In the photograph, Mother is fifty-five years old, a new widow. They married soon after that picture was taken.

The two of them are in their mid-eighties. As he loses connection with the present, the rhythms and structures they have carefully built disappear. Their social life no longer punctuates their time. What orients my mother now is her husband's moods. When he is disoriented, in need of reminding, he is vocal about how much he hates whatever is happening. When he complains, she tries to make it better.

I can barely stand to listen to her try to talk him out of his dementia.

The two of them have been anchors in each other's lives. But nothing my mother does can stop her husband from floating off. And *she* can't lose her bearings. Someone has to know the way home.

What Mother says about her husband is that he's "slipping." He "has good days and bad days." Then she changes the subject.

"Tell me about *you*," she says, her forced cheerfulness obvious. I comply, tell her about my life. But my deep concern about her dogs me every day.

Although Mother would never use these words, she feels like she's living in a cage. Not long ago she said, "I can't *go* anywhere. To the bank, to the hardware store, even for fifteen minutes. He follows me, wants to come with me. All I want is time by myself. He insists he's fine on his own, there's nothing the matter with *him*, but when I'm out of sight, I never know what will happen." She paused, then said, "No one understands!" exasperation stretching her voice. Although I knew it wouldn't do any good, I offered that there are others who do, other women and men her age who have a spouse with dementia, she just needs to meet them. The Alzheimer's Society has groups. I offered to call on her behalf, find out about caregiver support groups.

"You go," she said. "You know about these things."

She is both right and wrong. I don't know about living with a spouse with dementia from the intimate day-in-day-out experience she knows. I am a stepdaughter who lives a continent away, not a wife who lives in the same house.

But I am also a therapist who works with elders and their families as they struggle with unexpected and unwelcome experiences just like the one my mother and stepfather are in the midst of right now. My clients are caregiving wives, husbands and mid-life children who passionately tell me how everything that was familiar and predictable gets transformed by dementia, or Parkinson's, or ALS, who wonder how, *now*, to be a "good wife" or "good husband" or loving child. They face the same complex, thorny puzzles my family does, puzzles that expose behind-closed-doors details, that rearrange who helps whom for what. My clients would truly understand my mother's claustrophobia. I wish she knew them.

The mid-life children I meet struggle, as I do, to orient within family relationships now carried along by a disease process and caregiving efforts. They too find it hard to witness their parent changing, struggle to figure out what works now. They don't know how to believe the family will somehow be all right. Trusting their parents will successfully navigate this journey can be a stretch. Sometimes they believe their decisions and planning are better than their parents', take over tasks without permission.

They might decide Dad can't be counted on to pay the bills or take care of the car, and act, hoping to fix the problem. Their actions often fail to respect parents' routines and rituals, history of solving myriad problems, ways of honouring a personal contract about "sickness and health." Even when mid-life children act with the best of intentions, their actions backfire unless their parents' marriage is respected.

Older parents — with or without dementia — want similar behaviour from their children: experiences that celebrate what hasn't been rearranged by aging and illness, acceptance of illness and caregiving. Until they ask and give permission, few want their children to direct them how to proceed, or to rearrange their life. In most mature marriages, more-well spouses figure out how to work with dementia-related changes until they can't anymore. Their children need to exercise respect and careful timing when they open conversations about how to make the future easier.

Clients with dementia teach me about being lost. They show me their search for clues that remind them of roles, customs, professional training, well-known aspects of their earlier life that offer still-familiar ways to converse, act. In a session, a woman with dementia who has a history of entertaining and caring for others might take the lead, ask after my family before I ask after hers. If I follow her rather than reorient her, she exercises enthusiasm and empathy, gives me advice. I have learned from her that questions that used to open useful conversations now confuse her. When she's the question-asker, she's no longer lost. She's operating within a sphere of competence.

Like many of their friends, my mother and her husband are hesitant to hire "outsiders" to help them, except with outside tasks: lawn-cutting, gutters. Thus, my siblings and I were surprised when Mother, after stating testily that there's "nothing the matter with *my* mind," agreed to hire someone to help with her husband. For a month now, Helen, a woman in her forties, has arrived three days a week to help with housework and tend to my stepfather. He likes her.

My mother is right about her own mind: it's sharp and vibrant. But her eyes and energy aren't. Her house become dusty and sticky; meals miss key ingredients; she yearns for relief from her husband's constant "Where are you? What are you doing?" We children have discussed ways for her to go for lunch with friends, to her hairdresser's, into her room to take a nap. Until now she has insisted she'll handle it by herself.

"I went to the grocery store alone this week," said Mother over the phone. "Imagine that! Helen was here."

My shoulders dropped in relief. But days later, they tightened up when I heard Helen had asked for money for a sick daughter and my stepfather had given her a hundred dollars. They tightened further when I learned she'd asked for a loan; her husband was out of work.

"Gotta be careful about that, Mother. How much did you loan her?"

"A thousand dollars. She said she had no money for food. She has three children to feed. He'll get work soon, don't worry."

"I'm not worried about him. I'm worried about you and your generous heart."

"Oh I know, dear."

A week later Mother let my brother fire Helen.

As dementia takes over more of my mother's married life, my sense of worry about her deepens. Worry about her isn't new to me: it's rooted in the powerless panic I felt when I was nine years old and watched her grieve the loss of my sister, her youngest child. It's fuelled by her breezy attitude about safety and money. She has always been strong, feisty, and still is. The ever-tighter reins on her life, however, are strangling her signature light-heartedness. Gone is her enjoyment of the man she married: he drove the car, went to parties, played host, paid bills, fixed things. In his place, a changeling. A sense of captivity. She knew how to be a wife of someone who acted like a husband. Now she grasps at who she is. As his dementia worsens, she is pushed into an unexpected and foreign world. She is lost, too. And my need to protect her from distress and despair is fierce. When this desire erupts, I have to wrestle myself to the ground. I don't want worry to be my primary bond with my mother.

My visits to their home happen several times a year: winter, Mother's Day, late summer, her birthday. And when it's the only way I can calm my fear that she will die caring for her husband, I fly east. Sometimes one sister or another joins me and we calm each other's worries.

"What a surprise," says Mother when we announce a visit. "How did you get time off work?" She has no idea our bellies boil with anxiety.

During a recent visit, Mother reassured us she was fine. But her voice and face were serious. She'd lost more weight, didn't invite friends over much, rarely bought new clothes.

"What difference does it make?" She shrugged. "We can't go to parties. He can't handle it. It's enough to make a girl feel old."

My chest began to ache. I needed her to be spirited.

"He doesn't even know me most of the time, you know."

"Yeah, I noticed. That must be awful."

A few nights ago my older sister arrived for the weekend. We offered to cook. Mother announced we needed to "dress for dinner"; she wore fancy black slacks and a sparkly red top. We put on "dinner clothes." Mother asked for help with her eye makeup; she no longer saw well enough to apply it without looking like Bette Davis after a bad night. Dressed and coiffed, she looked like the woman she used to be. We waited in the living room for her husband. My sister made the drinks.

"What's taking you so long?" Mother shouted toward the hall.

"Nothing!"

She turned to us. "See what I mean? It's like this every night. He doesn't want dinner. I think he's forgotten how to eat. He gets up without eating, without saying a word, calls the dogs, goes to bed." She sighed. "But let's have fun. You're here and that's what's important."

"Want another martini, Mother?"

"Why not? This is cause for celebration, isn't it, the two of you being here at the same time?"

Moments later, with urgency in her voice, Mother shouted, "Darling?!" She turned to me, brows furrowed. "What do you suppose he's *doing* in there?" Then, "No need to check on him, he'll just yell. I think we should just sit down. Maybe he'll turn up. Maybe not."

We three were eating when we heard his footsteps and turned to welcome him. We stared. Silence. He was dressed, head to foot, in his officer's uniform from World War II. Hat, jacket covered with insignia, even a sword. He walked to the table, saluted and sat down.

"Why *darling*," said Mother, "you look so . . . handsome." She glanced at Nancy, then me, shrugged, raised her martini and said, "Bon voyage." She offered us a soft smile.

As he nodded to each of us and greeted us with a serious expression on his face, we knew he was on board a ship. We were his dinner table partners.

"I don't think we've met," he said to me, holding out his hand. I shook it and introduced myself. He nodded at Mother, who sat at the other end of the table. She introduced herself. He wiggled his eyebrows and winked at her, then turned to my sister. A smile spread across his face. He placed his hands on the edge of the table and leaned toward her.

"Peaches! How did you get on board this ship, you naughty girl?"

My eyes went wide. Mother's too. Peaches? Who was *Peaches*?

My sister didn't miss a beat. "Oh, you know me, I can be *very* clever," she said, her voice husky. He laughed. They bantered about ports of call. Mother and I watched, fascinated. He looked so happy, pleased with himself, delighted in this moment. Nancy was at her best: she was Peaches.

Moments later he winked, nodded to Mother and me and announced he had work to do. He stood, saluted, turned on his heel and walked toward the bedroom. Dogs growled, jockeying for space on the bed. His plate sat on the table, food untouched.

We sat in silence for what seemed a long time. Mother shook her head slowly from side to side. My sister and I held our breath.

Then, almost in concert: "*Peaches*?"

My sister's face wore a huge grin. Mother's too. Our laughter emerged in whispers. Mother got up and closed the bedroom door. She returned to the table, laughing out loud.

Her hand was over her mouth as she sat down. "Oh *dear*, oh dear, dear, dear, my poor husband." Tears now ran down her cheeks.

She turned to my sister. "Thank you, daughter. You were magnificent."

My mother's face, I realized, was relaxed. For this moment, she knew where she was, and her husband knew where he was.

Driving Lessons

Three weeks ago I decided to drive my eighty-two-year-old mother and even older stepfather to a family event in South Florida. The weekend now over, the three of us are again seat-belted in their frightfully old and beat-up white Mercury station wagon. I am behind the wheel. My stepfather sits next to me in the passenger seat; Mother is in the back. I can see her face in my rear-view mirror.

The car I'm driving is a vehicle Mother and her husband bought more than ten years ago, and they haven't taken good care of it. All five of their dogs are welcome in this car, and it smells like it. It has its share of dings and dents inside and out, including a crack in the front windshield that causes me to squint every once in a while. They don't think it's worth it to keep the car tidy and clean. The reassurance I needed on the phone a week ago was that the car would be serviced, especially the tires and brakes checked, before this trip. Mother said, "Oh, of *course*, dear, we'll get it all fixed up for you."

Because of its huge size, they call this vehicle the Queen Mary.

I detest this car.

Today we retrace our path back to South Carolina, where Mother and her husband live. This means heading north for several hours on Interstate 95 through Florida, turning northeast into Georgia and finally heading toward the shores of South Carolina. The sun-drenched retirement community where my mother lives is not an easy place to access by car or plane. It is near the Atlantic Ocean, on a river that joins the sea. Around it to the north, south and west are miles of scrub pine, lowland marshes and meandering waterways. The swampy lowlands are busy with wildlife and bugs. Obeying the commands of this geography, the roads jerk one way then another. To drive these roads after dark is to grope through pitch. Mother's community, an active and beautiful town centre on a glistening bay, has glorious antebellum homes, a seductive main street and seemingly endless strip malls; it takes at least five hours for any of their children — seven of hers and four of his — to get to them. For nine months of the year, the weather feels, to my body, like an inferno.

Tomorrow morning early I will begin my fifteen-hour hopscotch by limo and plane and taxi to get back to my home in Vancouver.

I wasn't going to go to this gathering. Who, after all, can afford to fly from British Columbia to South Carolina for a four-day lark? Certainly not me. While my times with family are precious and I never have enough of them, given the expense — often a thousand dollars — and orchestration required to rearrange my teaching schedule and clients, I rarely make spur-of-the-moment trips. I have to work hard to arrange a week or two, enough space to have real *time* with my mother and absorb the time zone and plane changes that are part of manoeuvring my way to her house.

The real reason I am on this trip is to keep my stepfather from being behind the wheel of a car. In the last several years he has had what Mother describes as "minor accidents" and "close calls." I don't categorize these mishaps so generously. Every time I hear about one of these "minor" dramas, I am left with an icy fear that my mother will die in this very car.

I decided to "chauffeur" them, as my mother calls it, after she told me on the phone that she wanted to go to this family event but couldn't. Her husband, she explained, "isn't up for the drive." Taking the train would be awkward; it takes too long and involves changing trains. They'd have luggage; she was sure he would have trouble navigating. She "could probably do the drive" herself, she offered, "if he will let me." What she failed to take into consideration when she said this was her macular degeneration, which has steadily removed her peripheral vision and left black holes in her sight.

In the background during this call, I heard my stepfather's booming voice: "There's nothing the matter with my damn driving. I'm *fine*. *I'll* do the damn driving!"

Mother put her hand over the phone. "No, dear, I don't really want to go. We'll just stay here."

I knew what would happen: Mother would tell everyone they wouldn't be at the event. Then my stepfather would wear her down until she agreed to go. At the eleventh hour they would get in the car and head south. On that day I would call Mother from British Columbia, not get an answer for six hours and figure out they were on the road. My sisters and probably my oldest brother would do the same thing. Then all of us would wait for a call from a state trooper after he pulled one of our business cards from the envelope in Mother's wallet that says *Call in an emergency.*

I thought about this scenario for two days, then called Mother to say I'd decided I wanted to go to this event. "I'll fly to Savannah, catch the shuttle limo to your house and drive you to South Florida. I'll do the driving." With this, there was a long silence. I got my stepfather on the phone and told him my plans, too. He was excited that I was coming east. When I told him I "really need to drive because I'm so pent up from my term of teaching and need an outlet," I heard him suck in. Then I added, "You can help me out by indulging my need to do a road trip. I really, really need your help here." He agreed. Reluctantly.

As we approach the north border of Florida and head into Georgia, I realize my stepfather has said little about my driving in the last hour or so. My shoulders are more relaxed than they were on the way south a few days ago; then, he offered a steady stream of advice on how to drive for the better part of the five-hour trip. But he now seems immersed in the scenery whizzing by his window.

"I made some sandwiches," says my mother. "We can stop anytime. Just find a rest stop. Or anywhere."

"How you doing back there, Mother?" I ask. "Anyone have to pee?"

In unison, both say, "No."

Suddenly I realize this car has no airbags. Wouldn't it be ironic if I were behind the wheel in an accident that kills my mother. I slow down and review the origin of my worries about my mother dying in a crash, as if it will inoculate her against harm.

It started several years ago, when she told me on the phone that her husband had a "little blackout, or something," and ran a red light.

"It's okay, no one was hurt, honey, don't worry. He just has a little bump on the head. He's *fine*." I knew that if *she* were fine, she wouldn't be telling me about the accident. I learned that three cars were damaged, including theirs. They were involved in a snarl of calls with their insurance agent.

"How are you doing with all this, Mother?"

"Oh, you know me." Nervous laughter.

That accident began my campaign to convince my stepfather to stop driving. I also worked on my mother; I wanted her to refuse to get in the car unless she or someone else was driving, because I believed he would eventually capitulate. When I suggested this, she told me in low tones that this would hurt his feelings, and besides, he got cranky when he didn't get his way and she didn't like being the target of his frustration.

I kept at these conversations, especially when Mother and I had our late-at-night-after-he's-in-bed talks in their living room. Then she whispered to me that she just *couldn't* do what I wanted her to do.

"So you'll die in a car crash? Is that it, Mother? Is that how you *want* to die? He's got dementia. His judgment is suffering. His capacity to navigate a six-lane freeway isn't what it used to be!" I knew I sounded frantic, pleading, and that she would ignore everything I was saying because of it.

She shook her head and said over and over again, "You just don't understand," and it was true, I didn't and still don't. I am not married to him and she is. This is her man, and I have learned over the years that no matter what, she will stand by him.

Three months after the "little blackout," their car repaired and insurance claims settled, they decided to take what turned out to be their last major driving trip. They wanted to visit family in Texas, which meant driving on the conveyer belt that is the interstate road system of the United States: four, six, sometimes eight lanes of traffic, often going in excess of eighty miles per hour, cars weaving in and out of lanes, moving acrobatically within inches of each other's bumpers.

For the most part, Mother was through with trips like that, but her husband wasn't. Somewhere in Texas, so the story goes — the one I heard through the family grapevine, not from my mother — they "went off the road," crossed the median, scooted in front of oncoming traffic, and eventually stopped, now headed north on the shoulder. Two "very nice" highway patrolmen showed up within minutes. They checked out Mother and her husband, discovered they were unhurt, helped them get back to the southbound lane and waved them on their way. It's likely none of the children would have known about this, had Mother not been so visibly shaken when they finally arrived at their destination. The story burned like wildfire from one kitchen phone to another.

This close call stirred most of their children into more action about their driving. We sounded exactly like the myriad daughters and sons in my workshops, gnawing on the bones of parents' driving habits and living in a personal hell of worry related to possible deaths, lawsuits, lives tossed up in the air with an absent-minded turn of the wheel. My sisters and youngest brother joined the campaign to talk with Mother's husband, but no one was successful. When we checked in with each other, we shared a sense of reprieve when a week went by without another accident.

Only months after the driving-to-Texas incident, there was a moment that changed everything for me. That day my sister Nancy and I, mid-way through a visit to Mother, were in the car with our stepfather. She was in the back, I was in the front passenger seat. We could see Mother needed a break from her husband's need for attention and assistance; she needed a few hours alone in her own home, released from taking care of him. We concocted a list of errands and told him we needed his help picking out new lawn chairs, getting gas and buying groceries at IGA.

After a half-hour in Kmart, we approached the freeway. Despite signs that said in huge red letters WRONG WAY, my stepfather turned the station wagon left rather than right. I saw oncoming traffic and my heart froze. As calmly as I could muster, I said, "I want you to do something right *now*. I want you to do a U-turn. Now. Please. Quickly." My hands were headed to the wheel to pull us off the road when he shouted, "Oh!" and executed a perfect U-turn. Moments later, three lanes of traffic raced by.

"Thanks," he muttered.

I pulled down the visor to see my sister's face in the mirror. Her eyes were wide. "Jesus!!" she mouthed.

After that I have never again gotten in the car with him if he is sitting behind the wheel. I told him why: I said I just couldn't. "It goes against my personal ethics," I said, appealing to him, "to contribute in any way to a likely accident that could hurt or kill my mother, or me, or you." He has argued with me, but I have stood my ground. My conviction is rooted in terror.

Because of this, visits since then have had a predictable standoff: The two of them and I, dressed to go out for dinner, stand by the car. No one opens a door to get in. My stepfather holds the keys tightly while he peppers me with adjectives: feminist, ridiculous, rigid, silly woman. Mother shifts from foot to foot, leaning one moment toward my quiet refusal, the next toward her husband's insistence. My heart thumps around in my chest. I know how much she hates my doing what she wishes she could do — refuse him.

The outcome has been varied. Twice he insisted in loud tones that my mother climb into the front seat; she obeyed as she tossed me pleading glances. Unable to figure out whether she wished I would try to stop him or would just stop refusing to cooperate with him, I watched him gun the motor and turn too quickly into busy traffic. Standing on their front walk, I prayed out loud, then went into the kitchen to make my dinner.

But not long ago during one of our "driving duels," he threw the car keys at me and grumblingly clambered into the passenger seat. On both occasions, the drive to the restaurant was marked by relentless instruction about how to drive, from *both* of them.

Mother started with "There's a stoplight up ahead. It turns from yellow to red quickly, so don't run the yellow light."

He was right behind her. "This is a speed zone. The damn cops will nab you. Watch *out*! Nutty woman!"

"Now, there's no need to talk that way to her, dear."

"Mind your own damn business. Slow down, damn it, can't you read the speed limit sign?"

"Honey, turn left two blocks before the restaurant so you can find parking. It's always packed at this time of night. I park behind the bank."

As they nattered at me, I told myself over and over that it was best to say nothing, even thank them for their input. Arguing or reminding them I had been visiting their community for over twenty years and knew the roads and parking places well would go nowhere. But what I longed to do — and oh, how vividly I imagined doing this — was stop the car at the next stoplight, fling my door open, leap out and run down the street, arms waving, screaming loudly while they gawked, paralyzed with wonder.

During those evenings, I knew that how I handled my stepfather during the drive would determine how well the next few hours would go. If my mother thought I could enjoy her husband even though he was "not himself," she warmed up and happily carried the evening. If I was at all solemn, she withdrew, which meant he and I had to carry the evening. We had some very awkward dinners.

It's amazing to me sometimes that we keep going out, but Mother loves good food and dressing up, so she continues to construct these Russian-roulette evenings.

Just before we begin the long journey through marshy terrain, I wonder how long it will take my mother to Get It — that her husband is significantly compromised by his disease, that his judgment cannot be trusted, *shouldn't* be trusted. So far I've been unsuccessful in convincing her to go to a group about Alzheimer's; she finds "those groups" and reading about dementia "too upsetting." I know she can't believe, doesn't want to believe, that being married to a man with Alzheimer's is part of her life.

I realize that *he's* been willing to talk about his changing health, just not his driving. When the two of us sit and chat about his life, which we do frequently, he's been willing to worry out loud about "getting lost" during the day and at night. He's described wrestling matches with a disjointed memory, despair about a mind that will no longer behave; he's told me how much he hates getting older in this way. I've tried to be as empathic as I can, but boiling underneath my concern for him is a red hot protectiveness of my mother. I know I will never forgive either of them, or myself, if my mother dies in a fiery crash.

My reverie is interrupted by a pull in the steering, so I turn into a gas station, feeling lucky that we are not deeper into the swamp, where there are almost no services. I walk around the car and look at the four tires, and see that one is going flat. Mother and her husband say nothing, but I see them exchange a glance. "Yep, there's a slow leak in that puppy!" says a cheerful attendant in dirty jeans and a torn T-shirt as he walks toward us wiping his hands. While he removes the tire, I buy three soft drinks and place one in each of their hands. It's almost ninety degrees both inside and outside the car and I'm thirsty. All three of us pop the tabs and take a long drink.

"Ah, that's so good. Thank you, daughter. Well, we might as well eat our lunch right here. This will be just *fine*, won't it," she says cheerily.

"I wonder how this could happen," I say. "I know you had the car tuned up and checked before the trip." I can tell by the worn-thin tires and Mother's pursed lips and wide eyes that they did no such thing. She lied to me when she told me the car had been tuned up. This damn junk heap hasn't been tended in years.

Mother gets the picnic basket out of the back seat and carries it to a worn table with attached benches under an oak tree. She takes out three sandwiches wrapped in plastic and a bag of potato chips. I tell her it's amazing that she got all that food together from a motel room, and she grins at me, obviously pleased at her own ingenuity. Over lunch we compare notes about one relative then another. My stepfather gets up and walks toward the mechanic working in the garage. About half an hour later the gas station attendant hollers, "She's ready to roll!" and we climb back into the hot car.

"Damn hot roads. They wreck perfectly good tires, you know. They should fix these damn roads," grumbles my stepfather.

"How much did it cost, dear?"

"Too damn much, that's how much."

Two hours later, within seventy-five miles of their home, the car begins to pull to one side and I know another tire is collapsing. As I pull onto the shoulder of the two-lane highway, Mother shoots me a worried look in the rear-view mirror. We are on an arrow-straight leg of asphalt in the middle of the wetlands. There are no streetlights, no services, no buildings. I open the windows, turn the engine off and put my forehead on the steering wheel for a moment.

My stepfather pokes me in the ribs. "What's the matter?"

I say nothing, but get out to look at the tires for the second time in three hours. I walk all the way around the car and stand by the driver's seat door. "Another flat tire. And no spare," I say through the window.

My mother looks at her lap. My stepfather looks out the window, seemingly studying the ditch by the car.

"Oh dear, what will we do? Here we are, in the middle of nowhere, and we don't have one of those modern mechanical phones, you know, the ones that run on batteries." I can tell she's worried. I didn't pack my cell phone. Dusk is settling in, and the few-and-far-between drivers are turning on headlights. They whiz by so fast the car sways in the air pressure change.

Suddenly my stepfather gets out of the front seat, goes to the back of the station wagon and opens the trunk. He yanks out the tire that first went flat, bounces it onto the dirt by the car, then rolls it to the edge of the asphalt.

"What are you doing?" asks my mother, a thread of fear in her voice.

"I'm going for help. I know what to do. It's just a flat tire. I can at least do *this*!" He shoots me a look that says *Stay back, girl.*

Mother pleads with him from the front seat. "No, no, honey, please don't do this. Someone will come along. The police patrol this road. They will come to help us. Remember that time we ran out of gas not far from here. Please, please get back in the car."

They argue for several minutes, but he is staring resolutely down the road. I make my eyes follow his, now see what he sees. A car is approaching. Its headlights get brighter and brighter. My stepfather tips the tire against his leg, leans out into the road and begins to wave his arms wildly, like a windmill. The car slows, stops. I cock my head to look at the driver. A black face is leaning toward him as he approaches a green Pontiac. The window of the passenger side slides down.

A voice: "Trouble, sir?"

My stepfather pushes his face into the man's open window. I see a young man in an army uniform. My stepfather, who has a history in the military, now salutes. He tells the driver about the flat tire.

"No trouble, sir. We'll have this fixed up in no time. Get in." With that, my stepfather climbs into the front seat of the Pontiac and, without looking our way, slams his door. The car guns it. Red tail lights disappear.

Astonished and silenced, Mother and I sit in the front seat, staring straight head. Two cars zoom by. Neither stops. I reach over and lock her door, then mine. We sit in stunned silence for about two minutes. Night is arriving; Mother and I turn into silhouettes. Outside, the wetlands stretch craggy and black. I turn the engine on to open the windows; maybe there's a bit of a breeze.

"Well," Mother says slowly, "we may never see him again." Then, starting somewhere deep in her throat, a chuckle. She tries to stop it and can't. It bubbles into a chortle, then a full-faced laugh. I stare, amazed, fascinated. With increasing abandon, Mother laughs and snorts. It's impossible to not join her. "He doesn't even know who he is, let alone where he lives. Or where *we* are. Who knows where he'll end up," she says and then laughs even louder. Tears are now running down our faces; we wipe our noses with Kleenex. "Oh *dear*," she spurts, but she still can't hold it together. More laughter. She takes a deep breath and says, "I think this calls for a drink. Would you like a glass of wine, daughter?"

With that, she reaches under her seat and pulls out a bottle of red wine she'd tucked under there when we left the motel. I grab two plastic glasses from the picnic basket and open the wine with a corkscrew.

As I pour each of us a glass of merlot, Mother and I are still laughing. Our plastic glasses click in a toast. "Ah," she says, "to my husband, wherever he is," and then she starts to laugh again. She straightens her shoulders and settles in her seat. I turn on the radio and fiddle with the dial until I find some jazz.

Over the next couple of hours, until a state trooper comes along (as Mother knew he would) and drives us into town, we listen to the jazz station, finish the wine and talk. Every few minutes Mother breaks into a free-wheeling laughter that makes me smile so much I feel my face stretch.

Voice-Over

"Oh *hello*, dear. Aren't you sweet to call. I know how busy you are."

My mother's voice is bell-like as she answers the phone. I know without looking at her that her eyes are bright and she is smiling. Within seconds I will be able to tell which of my three older brothers is on the line.

All three call her every afternoon between five and six. Conversations last about five minutes. Although they sound similar, her queries about each son's wife, children, grandchildren reveal who she is talking with.

"Oh, don't worry about me, honey, I feel great. Your four sisters are a wonderful SWAT team. We're all doing just *fine*. I'm sitting here with my cocktail. Tell me more about *you*, dear, your vacation."

I close my eyes, lower the back of my head onto the love seat near Mother's bed, listen to her voice swirling flirtatiously into eddies, tumbling over familiar family stones. After a little bit I stand, join my sisters in the living room.

Mother won't tell her sons she's not been out of bed all day. She won't say her vodka tonic sits untouched on her bedside table because the smell makes her feel nauseated. Or that an hour ago, her four daughters helped her sit up, poke arms into the sleeves of a fresh nightgown, wash her face and hands, brush her hair, put on lipstick, rouge and Je Reviens perfume, and shut off the TV. She has called the names of her four dogs, who nestle close to her sides.

All of this, to talk to her sons.

While she's on the phone, we four daughters sit in her living room. Occasionally we cluster at her bedroom door; we know her macular degeneration means she can't see us. We shake our heads at the music in her voice.

Some days her sisters and grandchildren call, too. By six o'clock, Mother is exhausted. I unplug her phone. Her eyes close and she sleeps for several hours.

The late-afternoon "cocktail calls" began a few weeks after the news was out that our eighty-eight-year-old widowed mother had been diagnosed with a fast-moving cancer. Soon, everyone in the family knew there was no cure and that she would be dead in a few months. Treatment might add a bit of time, but when she heard about the debilitating side effects, she decided to "just die at home with her dogs nearby". This news meant Mother and her children, none of whom live within 500 miles, had many phone conversations with one another. Mother had made it eighty-eight years without a serious health problem. This, her first, would be her last.

Her sons decided it was time for a final party and went to visit her right away, "while she still has energy." Although her skin already had an orange tint, as her oncologist had predicted, her leopard-print pants and gold-sequined top glittered in candlelight. My brothers took many pictures. There was Mother: stunning, girlish, smiling, arms around middles, glasses held high. They announced they'd likely not be back until the funeral. Mother nodded. "You three have such busy lives, even though you are retired. I don't want you travelling all this way to get to me."

In contrast, my three sisters and I left our work and families, travelled long distances, moved into Mother's house. We went to take care of her until she died, her house sold, all estate work finished. We tucked into empty bedrooms, laughed about living together for the first time since we were teenagers.

For weeks now, we have been doing the hard, intimate work of figuring out how to be together and to care for a dying mother. This has not been easy. There is no glitter.

Last week at 6:30 a.m. I walked across Mother's living room toward coffee. A greenish morning light glowed through the curtains, making the room look like an aquarium. My three sisters were already awake, sitting in easy chairs, sipping coffee, laughing.

Getting up early is essential in South Carolina in summer. The temperature hits 90° Fahrenheit by ten o'clock, so we seek the flimsy, fresh breeze of dawn through open French doors. In the air, a wash of sultry perfume from Mother's gardenias.

As I poured coffee, I heard whispering:

"*What's the matter with her?*"

"*Grumpy.*"

I turned slowly, walked toward my sisters.

"Good morning, sunshine," Nancy, the oldest sister, chortled from where she was tucked into a barrel chair.

I nodded to her, turned, headed back to my bedroom. "Be out in a minute."

Tears were running down my face.

The day hadn't even started and I felt raw, no skin. I had no voice, no words. I hadn't slept, dreamt Mother was wandering, pleading, "Don't let me die, don't let me die." Three times I'd gone into her room to check on her. I shut my door, put on sacred choir music, sounds that soothed, provided paths through pathos. I knew nothing remained untouched in this death bunker. My history grabbed at me.

My sisters' comments about my morning moods and behaviour had hurt. Why couldn't they let me be who I was? I wasn't hurting anyone. I hated being social in the morning, didn't wake up chatty, cheery. If I could buck up, be more bouncy, it would save me a lot of hassle, but I just didn't have that part of Mother in me.

When we were children, as Mother poked into one child's bedroom then another, herded us to breakfast and out the door to the school bus, she sang, chatted, laughed easily. When I didn't mirror her mood: "Uh-oh, you're in one of your *moods*!" My morning behaviour had long been the butt of family jokes.

After the party my brothers arranged, Mother tried to keep the awkward business of her dying not just from them, with her voice and ebullient mood, but also from her daughters. For several weeks she reported over the phone that she was up and about, going out for lunch and to church.

Although my mother said she couldn't imagine what drew me to my work counselling elders and their families at the end of life, after her diagnosis she asked me about my work, told me she trusted me, believed I had "good judgment." I promised her I would soon be with her in person to make sure her wishes were honoured. I bought a one-way ticket.

My clinical training means I register changes in skin colour, energy, sleeping and eating in people. After I arrived I saw my mother's skin change colour, noticed her naps got longer every day and that she ate less every day. Her internist told me she wouldn't have pain or cognitive struggles, but would lose weight rapidly. "Fairly quickly, she will become weaker, more frail, will want to sleep a lot. She'll likely find the hardest part is the orange skin and the hives. Almost nothing will stop that."

Not long after I arrived, a close friend of Mother's called. She'd heard about the short time frame, wanted to hold a luncheon, gather old friends. "We want to make sure your mother knows how special she is!"

That day, I helped Mother choose an outfit that would mute the colour of her skin. While plates of tomato aspic, chicken salad, Italian bread and butter appeared and friends chattered, Mother and I sat side by side. I grabbed her left hand, pulled it into my lap and held it tight. Her friends focused on me, asked about my "visit," commented on the heat, hoped I'd enjoy my time. No one looked at or spoke to my mother. She ate nothing, said nothing. I wished I could transform her friends into storytellers who would talk about the years of friendship and laughter. Cry, say goodbye to their friend. I realized Mother couldn't use her magic voice on them because they could see her skinny arms and orange skin.

By the time we left, my throat was swollen with silence. Mother wouldn't see these women again. Everyone at the table knew this was a final gathering of their friendship. That luncheon marked the end of my mother's social life.

Since then she has accepted no calls from her friends. If they drop by, she won't see them, so they leave cards and flowers and food. No matter what I say or how I say it, I cannot talk my mother into welcoming her friends to her bedside.

Now, sequestered with four daughters who have become caregivers, Mother is forced to share with us her shame and embarrassment. No matter how hard any of us tries, nothing can make invisible skin the colour of mango, bones poking through muscles, hives that demand nails scratch until skin weeps and bleeds.

It has taken time and patience for my sisters and me to orient to Mother's two worlds: the one behind closed doors and the one she presents over the phone. Initially this felt crazy-making. We wanted her to be real, hoped at least some of her vulnerability and frailty would leak into her voice tone and spoken words. But no. The evening calls transport her. She wants makeup, coiffed hair, a fresh nightgown, a cocktail nearby, her dogs. It's taken weeks to find any modicum of comfort with this discrepancy. It feels like tightrope-walking.

The cocktail calls have become a ritual that punctuates the day as poignantly as the sun coming up. When the phone rings, despite the smell of death in her room, Mother's Pied

Piper musical voice leads every caller into her woods, a place where they are seduced into thinking about themselves rather than her death. She doesn't want to think about it, so why should anyone else? When Mother had only a few hours of energy a day, her two sisters, also in their mid-eighties, insisted on visiting. Mother told us to get her ready. We daughters chose colourful clothes for her, dressed her, put on makeup, made up beds, prepared meals. I so hoped the three of them could experience an enclave in which they felt safe.

If Mother's goal was to make everyone pretend she wasn't really dying, the weekend was a success. She and her sisters sat at the dining room table together, laughed, drank cocktails in the living room, chatted about old times, children. The mood was effervescent. All three told me how important it was to be upbeat. When I saw each privately weep, they said the same thing: "It's too sad to share this."

When her sisters left, one rolled down the window of the cab and called out to my skinny orange mother, who stood on her front porch leaning into her daughters, "You look great, terrific!"

A day later, Mother summoned the Episcopal priest to her house. Again, her orders were to get her ready, then to leave them alone. We ironed an outfit she approved of, fixed her hair, put on makeup and helped her get to the sofa in her living room. There, she leaned back, folded her hands and took a deep breath. When the priest came in, Mother smiled and shook his hand. He sat down next to her. We heard her voice through the walls. It was plump with music.

After the priest left, we went into the living room. "Mother," I said, "you flirted with the priest."

I pull on my knowledge as a counsellor to understand my mother. Many of my clients have expended effort in leaving behind their past and turning toward their future. They have taught me that the human heart takes its own time making sense out of what's on life's plate. Although I know it takes time to embrace the juggernaut of death, this awareness offers context but no comfort. I am stretched by my mother's death. I know that her need for privacy and desire to control who knows about her intimate life is not unusual. Nor is her need to arrange and preserve attractive images of herself. Like many, she hasn't found aging interesting. She hasn't pondered death, loss. Instead, she has focused on the positive. Her public trademark has been her charm, verve, sparkly costuming, laughter.

But this woman I see every day is my mother, not a client. And I am with her morning and night, watching her unravel and pull herself like a rabbit out of her own hat.

So much of what Mother is doing has nothing to do with me and why my sisters and I are here. We came, we tell ourselves, to walk beside her. With us she's grateful, apologetic, hesitant, embarrassed, more available than ever before, a dramatically different mother than we've known. And we are amazed, grateful to know her in this way.

But every day, no matter how close we try to be, she moves further away, seemingly on a journey with no companions. We watch her eyes and wonder what she's seeing as she stares, smiling, out the window. And her fingers, which seem to twiddle as if she's creating something.

None of us could have foreseen how hard it would be to watch her leave, how much we would need her to reach toward us, acknowledge our lives. Instead, she spends her limited energy keeping those who cannot see her from knowing what we know. She wants them to remember her in her sparkle.

Even if she wanted to ease into another persona, she has little time to develop one.

———————————

Not long from now, my sisters and I will call relatives to tell them Mother is dead. Although we have phoned everyone regularly, sent daily emails with clinical details and poetic descriptions of changes in Mother's colour, weight, energy, interest in food, topics of conversation, we know they will say, "Really? She sounded fine last time we spoke."

River of Loss

Lightning slashed open the dark afternoon sky as I told my three sisters I was going crazy, had to get out of the house, go somewhere, anywhere. They stood in the front hall, their eyes wide, staring. They were afraid Mother would die and I wouldn't be there to tell them what to do.

"I'm just going for a stupid *walk*!"

"At least take the cell phone." Nancy pressed it into my hand.

"*No*! I want to be *alone*. I have to get away from all this death, all this . . . everything!"

And with that, I slammed the front door and strode furiously toward town. Within blocks, a deluge of rain, heavy and hot, cooling nothing. I raised my face to the sky and screamed, loud. Louder. Tears flooded my eyes.

I needed the faces and words of my two sons in British Columbia. Here in South Carolina, I felt imprisoned by the clutch of summer heat, confined by the day-after-day-after-day endlessness of taking care of my dying mother, waking and sleeping in her house, intimate involvement in the minutiae of her daily routines.

The relentlessness of the months-long caring had turned me into someone I didn't know or like. How deeply I wanted to be compassionate, gracious, flexible, able to roll with the undulations of her dying, able to take the next step as my mother and I wound down our relationship. Instead, the experience was curdling my grace. Stealing my humour. I'd turned inwards in ways I didn't recognize. Although I slept a lot, fatigue radiated from my bones. I felt alone even though I was surrounded by my three sisters — my closest friends. No matter how delicate and tender my conversations were with Mother, I couldn't soften the careful distance that marked this time. Although the care my sisters and I offered Mother was as thoughtful as any I'd known, I felt disappointed in myself.

After walking several miles to town, I surprised myself by seeking out a church. I pulled on the front door. Locked. Next to the sanctuary, a garden. I sat down on a marble bench, bunched my knees up like a seven-year-old, even though I was fifty-eight, wrapped arms around legs. Ragged breathing. Loud bird-like cries freed themselves from somewhere behind my breastbone. As more hot rain soaked me, I prayed. It didn't help.

The rain thickened, pounded harder. Thunder offshore. The gods were beating on my head like a drum.

My sisters. They would be frantic; I should go home.

Instead, I walked further away from the house, turned my face to the sky and shouted, "Bring it on, fucker!" My chest heaved. I gasped for air. Alien sounds pushed out of my throat. I looked around me. Not a soul in sight.

For the next hour, I walked the empty waterfront, talking out loud and listening to myself as if it were the first time I'd ever heard my own voice. I talked about my childhood. "Why am *I* the one doing all the crying? Again! Fuck! It's always been like that. 'Crybaby, crybaby,' my fucking brothers taunted after they punched and tricked. Jesus, Mother, what was the *matter with you* that you didn't *do something* when your sons were so, so mean to their sisters?" I had to stop, sit on a bench, hold myself. I heard my voice say, "Mommy, Mommy . . . Where is my Mommy?"

One deep breath. Two. Three. I knew what this was. Again, I was grieving the mother I wanted, needed and hadn't had. Not new. I'd studied loss and grieving, been in therapy, struggled to find words for one loss, then another. I'd learned no amount of knowledge could neutralize or erase what was going on in my chest and throat. I knew, I knew — when faced with a new loss, my heart would unearth previous losses from years, even generations, before.

Loss flows forward. It waits, sometimes generations, for acknowledgement, respect, expression. That's the way it works. Over time, if we give our losses the space and time they need to allow us to grieve, their enormity dissipates and we, fed by their lessons, grow a bit more into who we can be.

I knew all that. I just disliked the messy process.

When I reached the end of the waterfront walkway, I looked longingly at the wide arc of bridge that led from town out to the islands offshore. The road rose and disappeared into what looked like a cloud. I wanted to walk toward it, leave my thoughts behind, disappear into the soft white mist. But I couldn't move. Everything I wore was soaked, heavy. I wrapped my arms around a streetlamp pole and pressed my cheek to the cool metal.

A face. Real or imagined? An apparition?

It was Jack, my first "real" boyfriend, a young man I was entangled with for several years in high school and after, a tortured relationship of experimentation, passion, disappointment, fear. We held each other with a fierceness born out of trouble in both of our families, became each other's safe place when we were too young, too unequipped to provide such a profound gift to one another.

What was he doing here, now?

I closed my eyes, sat down on the curb by the lamp post, put my forehead on my knees.

He knew first that it — we — were too serious, too young, and called it off.

My mind flooded with images and sounds, not from 1964, when he ended our relationship, but from thirteen years later, when I ended my marriage and a new friend sat in my Vancouver living room trying to comfort me. I remembered my voice sputtering details about Jack, our relationship, my chest heaving with its desire to spill the story of him and my broken heart. My breath came in gulps. My words in clipped sentences.

When my tear-drenched words weren't about my husband but about a man before my husband, a name I'd never mentioned to my friend, her eyes had gone wide.

I told her how blindsided I'd been in 1964, how I had no longer been able see my future and had tried to jump out of Jack's moving car. The feel of his hand grabbing my shirt, yanking.

"He saved my life. Fuck. He saved my life," I said to her tearfully.

I plowed on, told her about staying up all night drinking and crying with my friend Rochelle, going over the details again and again.

And how I rarely mentioned Jack's name again.

Weeks after that dramatic night, I told my new friend, I'd met a new guy. When I was with him, the sadness lifted. I thought I was in love. He eventually became my husband, the one I was then leaving.

My friend's face was scrunched in wonder. "Christ! I thought we were going to talk about your marriage. Who – again — is *Jack*?"

The deep sadness I'd hauled around for thirteen years overflowed the banks of my own river of loss.

And here it — *Jack*! — was again, as I sat in the rain two miles from Mother's house.

"Not *you* again!" I shouted. "Go back into your cave! I've spent enough therapy dollars on you!" Then I laughed.

No escaping loss. Grief.

I wondered about my mother and her lineup of losses. Wondered if she felt a backlog now that she was at the end of her life. She'd tried so hard — for a lifetime — to "turn the page," not spend time and energy grieving, upsetting others. Her modus operandi was to have a good time. Now that she was at the end of her life, I could tell she was more open and soft than I'd ever known her to be. She spent time in silence in the end-of-day amber light of her bedroom, working her thumbs and staring into the west-facing window. She talked about her dead daughter, Dad. Had cancer captured her with her loss, made it impossible for her to turn a page or kick up her heels like a youngster? Was she being pushed to grow up a bit more, even now at this very late date?

I wondered if Mother inherited the sadness of her own mother, who lost *her* mother when she was a schoolgirl. Dad's mother, too, lost *her* mother when young. Both of my parents were raised by mothers washed in grief. No maternal guidance when the babies came. This grief, of course, would have leaked into my parents' marriage, influenced how they parented their own children. Children absorb their parents' pain, try to make things better, even without knowing why. My parents would have sensed the powerlessness and would have tried to make their mommies happy.

How little I talked with my dad, my mother, about the parenting they received, the grandparents they knew, couldn't know.

I couldn't ask my dad; he died in 1969 when I was twenty-three years old, before I'd formed any good questions. But he would have talked with me; he did things like that.

Tears streamed down my face. "Dad."

So many questions I'd have asked him. He and I talked about his illness, his fears, but not about his parents, childhood, feelings. I've pieced all that together by talking with his sisters, but it wasn't enough. I carried a sadness about my father impossible to integrate without hearing his stories.

During the whirlwind of activities that followed his death, I was robotic, attention riveted on Mother, my younger sisters, Dad's estate. He'd appointed me executor. I had to stay focused.

Only months later, when travelling with my husband in Europe, I sat on a camping chair in Venice, Italy, staring at the night sky, when a wall of water swept me into a wail that caused my new husband's eyes to go wide. I crumpled. "Dad, Dad, Dad."

It wasn't too late to ask my mother about her mother, about having no maternal grandmother.

———————————————

A hand on my shoulder. I looked up into Casey's face. Her eyes were filled with tears. She was soaked. She held out her hand, grabbed mine and helped me to my feet. "Come on. Time to go home now."

She put an arm around my shoulder. Our running shoes squished as we made our way home.

Part Three

Follow the Money

Barbara, a client I had known for several years, called for an appointment. "You're going to think I'm a nutcase. My mother and I are having weekly battles about her *purse!*"

Every week since her father died last year and her ninety-two-year-old mother moved into a nearby dementia care facility, Barbara had taken her mother out for lunch. What started out as a sweet ritual was turning into a nightmare.

As Barbara sat down her hands flew into the air. "She's driving me crazy. What is it with the fucking purse? 'Where's my purse? Where's my purse? It was just here a minute ago.' Every Monday when I pick her up to go for lunch, she acts like a maniac as she searches her room. 'Mother,' I say, 'You don't need your purse. I've got plenty of money.'"

"What does your mother say to that?"

"I'm not stepping one foot out of this room without my purse." She tosses everything off the bed, looks in the bathroom. She's frantic.

"Come on, Mother, it's here somewhere, but you don't really need it, do you?"

"Yes, yes, yes I do!" she yells.

The black leather purse with the loop handle always eventually turns up and the two drive to their favourite restaurant, where her mother orders the same meal — clam chowder and a side salad — every week. When the check comes they predictably argue over the bill.

"I have *plenty* of money!" says Mother, over and over.

The struggle with the purse and the check ate away at Barbara. Her voice stretched thin, she said, "My mother and I are at war over a purse with nothing in it."

"So what's in the purse?" I asked Barbara.

"*Nothing!*"

"Literally?"

"I manage her finances, so I check to make sure she's got a few bucks in case she wants to buy something on one of the trips out. She doesn't need to pay for lunch. She bought me lunch my whole life, and now she's old and it's my turn. I can afford it."

"So what's in the purse?"

"You're kidding, right?"

"No."

"Okay." Barbara paused, closed her eyes for a moment. "Her comb. Lipstick. Tums. A small wallet with twenty dollars in it. That's it."

"What's in the wallet besides the money?"

"Now you *are* kidding."

"No."

"Um, a driver's license that expired fifteen years ago. A membership card for the local garden club, also long expired. Her card for the Legion — Dad was in the service.

My brother's business card; he died four years ago. My name and phone number. A picture of her, Dad and me taken at Niagara Falls when I was twelve. And the twenty dollars."

"Tell me about the picture."

Barbara stared at me quizzically. "They're holding on to each other. I'm behind them peeking between their shoulders. It's cute. That was a good time. What does that have to do with anything?"

"If you were lost, how would you find your way back home, Barbara?"

"I guess I'd look for familiar landmarks."

"Me too. I wonder what your mother does if she ever feels lost — which is common with dementia. She *could* look in her wallet: There's her name. And proof she's been a wife, mother, gardener, member of the Legion. A mother who has enough money to take her daughter out for lunch."

Barbara looked hard at me. "My mother forgets who she is?"

"I don't know. But when we get old, we all want to know that we are — have been — somebody. Sometimes it's hard to hang on to all we once were. Your mother doesn't have to wonder, does she? It's all right there in her wallet. Along with the money."

Taking the time to respect what money means to other family members typically enriches conversations about finances.

When old parents or their children come for counselling, it doesn't take long before finances nudge into the conversation, discussions in which some parents espouse advice about fiscal responsibility: stand on your own two feet, pay your own way, support yourself and your family. All are common criteria for maturity. In terms of nudging children into a life where parents don't pull out their wallets to pay for a new outfit, a meal, grandchildren's sports activities, educational opportunities, they make sense. A certain amount of financial independence creates a valued psychological separation between childhood and adulthood, between child and parent. Given its importance, and the often bumpy process of achieving fiscal self-reliance, it's not surprising that money is a delicate and often explosive focal point in families. For many, talk of family finances is more private than talk of sexual activity. Even after children are paying their own way, sensitivity to how and if money flows between generations pulses on, often surreptitiously. Money winds itself around family power and dependence like seaweed. Especially when parents rely on their children for financial support, how money affects grownupedness in both older generations is complicated.

Children's awareness also increases as they register that their parents' money is beginning its journey to wherever it is going after they die. The hopes, fears, needs and promises of both generations awaken. Elders living too close to the line cut back, access resources designed to help, look toward children and other relatives. Grown children whose lifestyle has been supported by parents' resources — especially if benefits will cease when their last parent dies — pay special attention. This does not mean that family conversations suddenly start happening; it just means they should. Perhaps because it takes so much sensitivity and maturity to talk about this delicate topic, it's not surprising conversations are pushed ahead, even when doing so will enflame the future.

When conversations eventually happen, often in lawyers' offices, family members learn about — despite what a will says or stickers on the back of paintings claim — the emotion attached to parents' "stuff." In addition to what a lawyer lays out about the law, each person's stories and treasured promises now influence how personal items — china, jewellery, writings — are dispersed. Feelings of entitlement about stocks, land, houses boil up. As emotionally charged as this can be, adult children and their parents don't exchange stories about meaning unless they have to. Even parents with several frugal adult children may avoid talking about the one son who spends without reflection, even if his behaviour is a source of noisy family strife. A daughter who protects her father's right to enjoy his own nest egg may learn after their mother dies that her sister is frantic about how Dad is spending his own money, which she now calls "my inheritance." A newly widowed mother who always counted on her husband to manage finances tells her children their dad wanted everything divided evenly, only to learn that their oldest son was told he was to take over financial decisions. His younger sister may retort, "Well, if you're calling the shots on all the stuff, that means I'm *toast*! And I want his violin. I'm the only one of us who played music with him." When everyone knows and agrees with a parent's wishes — especially if they are reflected in the will — collective behaviour is more likely.

Every family member has a "money history" that influences their relationship with finances — their own and their parents' — and thus how they behave during discussions about money. These stories often are a clumsy snarl of personal meaning and hard-edged financial smarts.

Each member's history is part of the puzzle that unravels when old parents die.

Sooner or later, what money means becomes clear.

Sometimes failing to understand the meaning of money to another family member has far-reaching consequences. A fifty-four-year-old daughter, Jen, slumps in the chair opposite me as she shakes her head and mumbles how embarrassed she is. Her long-widowed wealthy mother has been paying a mortgage on her large house since she married thirty years ago. Mother also financed private school education for her daughters, trips to Europe — all things her mother had when she was young. All things Jen and her husband could never afford on his earnings.

"I didn't marry into wealth and my mother couldn't stand it. To be truthful, neither could I. And my husband figured out early on that Mother would make sure we lived in the style to which *she* was accustomed." A big sigh. "That's likely why he married me. God, I hate this!"

"And now your mother is unwell," I offer.

"Oh yeah. She's ninety, at the end. And when she dies, I'm hooped. My siblings have no idea how much Mother has propped me up. I'm the only daughter. My two brothers got help from Dad getting business careers off the ground. But Mother really wanted to redo her life in my life, and I didn't protest. Nor did my husband. My brothers know my husband has never made enough for us to live where we do, how we do. But nothing is ever said. Last week Mother told me she's been keeping tabs on how much she's doled out to kids and grandchildren, and the records are attached to her will — amounts that will be deducted from our inheritance." Tears run down her face. "Help!"

"What are you most worried about?"

"What if I have to sell my house? Fuck! I may have to go to work. God, I'm fifty-four."

I think about other mid-life children who have lived with a financial safety net that unravels as a parent or grandparent dies, whose financial literacy and management also didn't develop well. They, too, had a relative who opened their wallet so often that earning, budgeting, postponement of gratification, saving never became an integral part of their relative's daily life. Some clients — those who knew finances were, ultimately, their responsibility — grew up in a big hurry as their parents got to the end of their lives. Others, those who struggled with entitlement, often turned to siblings, aunts, or uncles to maintain their lifestyle. Which worked for a while. Until it didn't. These daughters and sons were hard to help. Loosening the stranglehold of entitlement takes humility, a trait difficult to activate late in life.

"You're not counting on an inheritance," I said to Jen.

"Ha! Well, sure, I'll get something. My mother's rich. But she's *still* paying my mortgage — I renewed it twice when we did renos. No matter how much she's given my brothers — and I have no idea — it's nothing compared to my tab. I guess you could say I got my inheritance early. Jesus. I feel like . . . a child."

The financial relationship between Jen and her mother, while it had stalled Jen's maturity, had been a trade between the two women: Jen accepted money to finance a lifestyle she'd enjoyed while growing up. To her mother, this was particularly important, especially because her daughter didn't "marry money." Although it was never expressed in words, Jen knew her mother needed her to be socially prominent, have grandchildren who went to private school.

It was important to visit often, express appreciation. She knew this contact allowed her mother to feel an intimate part of Jen's life. Jen and her family enjoyed a large house, private schooling, status.

Like many offspring of wealthy parents, Jen didn't consider seriously enough the long-term consequences of building a life around parents' resources, nor did her husband. The news that her mother's generosity was detailed in a ledger and that Jen's inheritance would reflect those numbers felt like a rude awakening.

"So all this is a surprise to you?" I asked Jen.

"Not exactly. I knew there would be some sort of evening-out of money, but — a ledger?! God. It never seriously crossed my mind that she would leave me less well off than I've . . . always been. She's invested a lot in the way I live. I guess I thought she'd leave me enough for that to continue."

"And you're sure she hasn't?"

"Yes. Well, not exactly. My oldest brother has helped Mother with investments. He told me what she's worth. It's a lot, but it won't be for me once the lawyer deducts what I now see I 'owe.' I should have taken Mother more seriously when she said, after a few drinks, 'The gravy train isn't forever.'"

My own consciousness about money exploded one summer while I attended a summer institute at University of California, San Francisco. Seminars addressed a wide variety of women's health issues, including financial health. I was thirty-six years old, a single parent, a university teacher. I was selected to attend the institute because of my research on mid-life women. The lectures and courses offered rich current information about women's bodies, psyches, families, lifestyles, choices. The impact of disability and illness was examined, the power of cultural differences explained.

I was mesmerized.

One course about older women and their financial situations still remains vibrant. How and why so many women end up poor at the end of their life was examined by sociologists, financial experts, therapists and authorities on gender behaviour. Older women held microphones and shared their understanding of how they'd ended up with so little after starting out with so much. Graphs and charts revealing changes in financial data over a lifespan glowed on huge screens. The cost of being old, sick and disabled was blatantly displayed.

There in the darkened auditorium, I felt my chest tighten, my skin go cold. Too fearful to take notes, I put my pen down and listened with my whole body. I'd never thought about these aspects of money.

Back then, I didn't worry much about money; I counted on my skill with budgeting, saving, planning. I had a decent job, received a bit of child support, knew how to make do. My father had taught me about compound interest, savings accounts, even a bit about investing. He'd showed how one stock he'd bought thirty years before had grown, told me to invest as soon as I had money to do so. But he died when I was twenty-three, before he taught me why to follow global news and financial data and the importance of diversifying.

He left each of his children the same amount of oil stock. I decided to leave mine alone, let it grow. This worked until the oil crash in the 1980s, a year before I went to San Francisco and listened to speakers talk about women and their money. Then, almost overnight, my stock lost all its value. I'd not been aware there was an oil glut that determined the worth of my stock. My investment counsellor may have assumed I didn't care much about my stock.

I lost the only money I had.

I felt ridiculous. I had no idea how to think about what happened, so I didn't.

Until that day in San Francisco, when I saw myself in the life-sized realities presented in story, graph, and research results. Like too many other women, I'd relied blindly on others to take care of something I didn't understand. I'd not paid attention. How easily I could end up like the women holding the microphones, talking about how their husbands had "managed all that," or had never worked because they believed they didn't need to, or had counted on an inheritance that didn't materialize.

My own financial trajectory — past, present and future — snapped into view. I grew up very quickly that day.

That summer, it was impossible for me to know that within ten years I would be counselling mid-life children and old parents as aging and illness shifted their relationships and spending priorities and introduced new, sometimes shocking, expenses. That I would watch old parents' faces flood with fear as they wondered out loud if there would be enough to get to the end. Mid-life children involved in care of their parents would ask if they should be reimbursed for out-of-pocket expenses their out-of-town siblings didn't have to worry about and Mother and Dad seemed to ignore. Sisters and brothers who sacrificed employment to care for parents would wonder if they should receive more inheritance than their less involved siblings. Parents and children alike, I learned, were living with the consequences of financial beliefs and habits developed usually long before frailty or illness arrived. In some families these pushed all generations to take responsibility for their own emotional and financial behaviours. In others, beliefs and habits undermined fiscal and emotional maturity, and tangled generations in heart-wrenching knots.

Sadie, seventy-four, and I first met when her husband was diagnosed with Alzheimer's and she had to take over the family's finances. Her husband Robert, seventy-six, a successful businessman, explained he "just couldn't track the figures anymore." Fortunately, Sadie knew the ins and outs of the family's financial situation. She insisted she wasn't like friends who'd trusted their spouse with finances only to discover after a divorce or death that their ignorance had devastating consequences.

Sadie's concern was not taking over the books. It was how money was spent.

Three of the four children, all successful professionals, she said, agreed that family money continue to be spent on good schooling for grandchildren, family reunions, gifts, a comfortable life for Robert and her. The youngest son, David, said he thought it was up to Robert to decide how to spend what he'd earned, but he himself didn't want it. Unlike his siblings, he'd dropped out of university, lived a careful, somewhat unpredictable life. His parents wanted him to have a better apartment, a better school for his young daughter. Only David lived nearby.

Sadie wanted to "make life easier" for this son. She began to deposit a "monthly allowance" in his bank account.

When David asked about it, she said it was the least she and Robert could do — he helped them with so much. His siblings lived too far away to do what he did.

"I thought it would make things better," she told me. "It didn't. All the goodwill seemed to drain out of our relationship."

When I first met David, he came alone.

"I don't *want* their money," he said with a sigh. "I just want *my* life. Not theirs." He looked straight at me. "This is not a new problem. It's just bigger now that Dad isn't at the wheel anymore."

"How much do they know about what *you* want?"

"I've tried. But it seems beyond them. Why would anyone want to scrape by?"

When he and his parents came for a session, David moved his chair next to his parents — he didn't want to meet his father's eye. Holding her husband's hand, Sadie outlined how David's lifestyle was causing "unnecessary conflict."

"I thought a bit of money that you could count on every month might mean life could be . . . smoother."

"Mother, please. I'm fine. We've been over this. You don't like the way I live, but I do."

Silence.

"Is it okay if we 'talk money' for a few minutes?" I asked. They all agreed.

I nodded at Robert. "I'd like you to go first. Please, tell me about you and money."

Sadie's eyebrows shot up, but Robert smiled at me. "I came from nothing. My parents had very little education, but they worked very hard to make sure my sisters and I had what we needed to get by. After high school, I had to make my own way. Oh, how I wanted to do better than they did! And I did. I went to school. Went to school some more. It took a long time, but eventually, I wasn't living like my parents anymore. I had money in the bank." He smiled at me.

"How proud you must have been. How proud you must be."

"You know, I was. Am." He looked at David, who was looking at the floor. "I didn't want my children to experience what I did." His brow furrowed. "So I sweated so my kids could have great schooling, a foothold in business, down payments."

"How much do your children know about this?"

"Some. But it feels . . . embarrassing. My parents . . ."

"So, when David refuses your generosity . . ."

David cut in. "But I can't accept what you two want to give me. It seems to take me in the wrong direction. Maybe I have to do what you did, Dad, . . . just *do it*, carve life out of what I've got."

Sadie grabbed her son's hand. "It doesn't have to be that hard."

"But maybe it does. I don't have much . . . ," he paused, "backbone." He looked at his father. "Maybe yours got so strong because it *had* to. Maybe I need to grow mine because . . . I have to."

"You are rejecting me."

"Dad, please. No, I'm trying to get on with my life. Mother, please, no allowance, no inheritance. I will be there for you two no matter what. It's what I want to do. I don't want you to pay me for picking up your prescriptions or taking you to the doctor. Give it to a charity. Please. I need to feel a bit of fire under my feet; then I'm good to go."

David was teaching his parents what it took for him to become more grown-up. To him, letting go of his parents' money represented a gain, while accepting it and depending on it was a loss. To grow, the risks involved in turning toward a gain must be greater than enduring the loss.

"Maybe your son wants to grow the strength you did?" I said, looking at Robert. "To feel the edges of life that you did."

"But he doesn't need to!"

"Maybe it's not about need. Or rejection. Maybe it's about creating a life, being a grown-up in this family."

For every David I've met, I've met four who admit their hunger to know how parents' money fits into their own future. "It's going to come to me anyway," some say outright. "Why bust my ass saving for retirement?" Or "They have more than they need and I have so little, what difference does it make if I take a little now?" The danger, of course, when money (even the promise of money) flows between generations without openness is that it can postpone becoming an adult who takes responsibility for one's own life, sometimes indefinitely.

How Touching

One December night, I held my forty-five-year-old son's arm as we walked down Trinity St. in Vancouver. We commented on Christmas lights glowing in clear dark air. The fleece of his jacket was springy under my fingertips. The warmth of his body came through double layers of fabric.

Later, with my grandchildren, little arms wrapped around my arms, legs, shoulders; bottoms plunked onto my lap; fingers reached for my fingers, stroked my hair; small bodies squashed close to read a book. I was ambushed by the calming delight of spontaneous, innocent touch, their warmth and smoothness, a blessing that relaxed, opened my heart.

In the last while, I retired from a long career as a university teacher. I've kept my therapy practice going. As part of my initiation to the life of the semi-retired, I've been exploring what one ninety-year-old client labelled "the world of the elderly young." He insists that after a career ends, much feels rubbery, tricky. We have to figure things out all over again.

This includes time, relationships, health, identity. Touch.

When I was a young university professor, I taught a required course about aging and families. My students were young, but headed toward work in health care settings where they would encounter oldsters and families. At that time, it was considered unusual if not foolish to teach courses about old people, but I did anyway.

As I tried to awaken interest in older people, students slumped in chairs and rolled eyes. I didn't earn their steady gaze until two things happened: they offered stories about old people in their lives, and they shared imaginings about who they thought they would be when they were old. Until then, words like *gross*, *disgusting*, *out there*, described their reactions to the world of the elderly. They assumed no one in their seventies, eighties, nineties cared much about being touched.

Link the words *touch* and *elderly* and what happens? Some people — not just university students — screw faces up, as if even the thought of touching an older person is *horrible*. I wonder how much of this disgust, so massaged by marketing, reflects a belief that touching, stroking, holding belong to the smooth-skinned and shapely, and certainly *not* the grey-haired. Seemingly, only a few types of attractiveness deserve touch. Such a narrow definition excludes most, especially those "of an age" who have stopped chasing advertising's promises.

"How does one get from where you are to there?" I asked my students, young men and women whose bodies sought and adored touch. Downcast eyes. A woman three rows back scribbled a note, laughed as she pushed it along a row of desks.

"I'm serious. Tell me what you think."

Silence. Then a voice, hesitant: "I can't imagine my grandparents having sex. They're kind of . . . dried out."

Someone gasped.

"So perhaps we need to use our imagination more as we age?"

Laughter, heads nodding. Then, discussion.

———————

As spouses and love interests divorce or die, it's easy to see how older people end up on their own, and to assume they are the ones who puzzle most, wonder if it's considered disgusting to touch an old person. But the wonder and worry is not just for seniors who have limited opportunities to (literally) bump into someone else. In my counselling practice with older people, I frequently learn from married seniors who share history, beds and rituals how much they, too, are troubled by when, if, how and from whom touch can happen — and by how and why it doesn't, shouldn't, can't. When is touch inappropriate? Is it wrong to go to bed with a friend's husband if his wife is demented and in care? Is it ridiculous to masturbate at eighty?

———————

Not long ago I talked with an older sister about touch and aging, a topic we hadn't yet plumbed. We tiptoed in.

"I've forgotten about my body," she said.

"How can you do that?"

"It's over. It's too painful to think about."

We described changes in our aging bodies, reminisced about men we'd known who we thought understood a woman's relationship to touch, then moved toward now: two older women on their own, no love partner in sight for years. Who touched us *now*?

For many years I used the term *dry spell* to describe times between love relationships, between times of holding and being held. Then, I'd felt like a juicy mango on a windowsill, waiting.

This, now, was more than a dry spell.

"I'm just . . . *not home* from my neck down. It's easier," said my sister. I felt the same sadness I do when other older women say those same words, told her that. "And you?" she poked.

"Your way may be easier, but I *am* still home, it's just — nobody comes to call. My hairdresser and massage therapist are the closest thing I have to sex in my life."

We laughed. But it wasn't funny.

This sister was the most luscious of the five Green girls: flirty and spunky, musical, fluid on the dance floor, ready to laugh, ever laying a hand on the thigh of the man sitting next to her, even if it was, as I later learned, my boyfriend.

In contrast, I was lanky, studious, serious. I waited rather than jumped in. Boys were attracted to my looks but made up stories about long-legged blond-haired girls they hoped were lusty and not so smart, stories that were a poor match for my personality. Every boyfriend I had, I'm sure, wanted to take my sister to bed. And I wanted my boyfriends to look at me the way they did her, wanted to enjoy flirting like she did. But flirting didn't come naturally to me.

We both struggled to figure out sex and sensuality. Only when much older could we talk about that, but those conversations cemented our trust.

In our recent conversation, my sister and I weren't talking just about sex; we were exploring the broad world of touch. We discussed the daily, meticulous attention she gives to her nails and long silver hair, how this connects her to her body. I asked about her touching her dog, Sophie, who cuddles and offers warmth generously. I told her I often watch her when I visit, am struck by the tenderness with which she plays with her dog.

"It's so safe, so unconditional," she said.

"Like Mother was with her animals."

Especially during her later years, our widowed mother was tender and touchy with her half-dozen dogs. She stroked and talked to them, honoured uniqueness in each, easily accepted their warmth, licks, snuggles. She wanted them around her at the end of her life, and there they were, curled around her body until days before her death.

It's well known that older people do better when they have an animal. As I write that, I think about the cat who came to me from nowhere, who sat on my back porch until I took her in, who stayed for two decades. A cat who tended me and my clients — climbed up, put her face close, purred into ears, crooned, *It's all right, it's all right*. She understood.

When I was young, I confused sexual touching with sensual touching, and because I did, I focused more on sexual intimacy than touch. This didn't serve me well. I couldn't discriminate between desire and sensual or soul-nurturing needs, and when I finally could I was unsure what actions I should then take. Comfort with that took maturity, courage and words that matched more nuanced aspects of touch.

In this stretch of my life, perhaps because I take more time with almost everything, my skin is more attuned, reaches into worlds of rough and smooth, hot and cold, busy and still, soft and hard, pulsing and quiet. It refuses to relinquish enjoyment of sensation. I attend to texture, silkiness of fabric on skin, air movement, temperature, sound vibrating near my body. Increasingly, my other senses want to explore the world: to hear more subtlety, view art with more sensitivity, enjoy flavours more fully. I am like a sea anemone, translucent filaments waving in water, reaching out to encounter, interpret, search for nourishment and find a future in what's nearby.

Years ago I dated a man who was paraplegic, had no sensation from the middle of his body down. One night, as we sat at the back of a theatre awaiting a movie, we talked about touch and desire.

"It's all about the brain. I'm sure you know it's the sexiest organ," he said.

"I do."

"The brain's use of imagination can be truly impressive." He paused. "Let me show you."

He took my left hand, which wore a black leather glove. I started to take the glove off.

"Let *me* show you. Close your eyes."

I felt him begin to remove the glove. Slowly. More slowly. So slowly I had to reach to tell if he was touching me at all. My focus zeroed in, then loosened, expanded. I felt tiny movements of hands over more and more of my body. Heat and desire crept up my thighs, across my breasts. By the time the glove was off — about six minutes later — tears streamed down my face. I knew I gleamed cherry red.

I opened my eyes, felt exposed, enthralled.

He smiled warmly. "See? Your brain took license with a tiny amount of data."

After the movie we discussed how invisibility results when people don't touch someone who "can't feel." This is compounded when seated in a wheelchair.

"To be visible and worth touching," he said, "one must be young, whole, vertical."

The hands of my massage therapist and hairdresser soothe my need for touch. Both have aged with me on this journey into being older. My massage therapist lights candles, puts on music, spreads warm oil on my body. Afterwards, I know where I end and the rest of the world begins. My body glows. Others can't look through me now. My hairdresser, who works with older women all day, hugs, presses warm palms into shoulders. He knows.

When my mother was dying, my sisters and I brushed her silver hair every day. Perhaps because of her long history with hairdressers and braiding the hair of four daughters, this touch was welcome, safe. We climbed onto her king-sized bed, sat behind her, propped her up, ran her hairbrush through soft waves. "Yes, oh yes," she sighed. Crown to nape, so slowly. Those moments of intimacy — a call in all of us answered.

Sometimes my granddaughter brushes my silver hair. I lean into her touch trustingly. Because I, too, brush her waist-length red hair, it's an exchange that fits us right now. At thirteen, she doesn't ponder why people who look longingly at her red hair wouldn't fix eyes on my hair. It wouldn't enter her mind that people wouldn't want to hug her grandmother, brush her hair. Not yet.

Not long ago a once-upon-a-time love interest arrived for a visit, during which we enjoyed walks, ice cream, salmon, cooking together, movies. We allowed the psychic and physical space we needed to be friends. The visit felt light, breezy. Then on the third afternoon he hugged me before he left to see a friend. Not the usual, perfunctory clasp, but long enough to feel the heat of hands through my T-shirt, fingers on back, thighs touching, lips, dry, warm, soft, pressed into cheek.

After he left, I felt unbalanced, falling backwards, Alice-like, down a rabbit hole into a world where everything was skin-to-skin. My body remembered. Everything. It reached out over years for moments moist, warm, athletic, poetic. Flooded with images and sensations, my heart thumping, I sat down.

That night I dreamt of a long, lean tiger, orange and black stripes against flattened blond grass, asleep and then awakening, blinking heavy eyes open, yawning, turning head and ears one way, the other, licking paws. Eyes clear, bright, surveying the horizon. Slowly, strategically, she rose to a stand, looked around, began to saunter across caramel-coloured ground.

I awakened. Oh, how I missed being held, feeling hands on my back, fingertips, lips. Warmth of body on body.

Tears spread across my cheeks.

I'd not seen this tumble into naked touch-hunger coming. I felt ambushed.

But perhaps this is how desire happens at this age. During dry spells, conservation requires carefulness, hesitancy, even blindness. If the weather suddenly changes, it's hard to believe the downpour.

I knew better than to embroider the afternoon hug, make it more than it was.

By morning I felt the soft snore of my sleeping tiger again.

Because of my work with mid-life and older people, even when unsolicited, I am told stories about aging, mainly by women. Sometimes these are about sex, body changes, dating, wondering if they've had their "last chance" at love.

One eighty-five-year-old woman who lived in a retirement complex told me about meeting a seventy-five-year-old man, a friend of a neighbour. During his visits, she and this man became friendly. Both were widowed. They swapped stories. Discovered they enjoyed crossword puzzles. Began to look forward to seeing each other. After her neighbour died, he continued to visit.

"I felt more awake than in years!" she told me. "Bought new clothes. Had my hair cut and coloured. My kids laughed — 'Mother has a boyfriend!' "

The night they drank wine and talked about bucket lists, he put his hand over hers, caressed the top of her fingers. He touched her hair, kissed her, called her "dear."

"I felt visible for the first time since my husband died."

Within days they were talking about a trip to Bali, a place both had dreamt about. When he began to spend nights with her, she believed the physical pleasure was mutual, thought he cared.

Plans for Bali took shape. Because she had a "fatter wallet," she told him it made sense that she pay for airfare and hotel and he, meals.

Once in Bali, she barely saw him, except when he came to the hotel to sleep. Upon return to Canada, he disappeared.

"That," she said, pointing up, "was my five-thousand-dollar roll in the hay." She paused, met my eye. "Is that what it takes for an old girl to be held?"

"I don't know."

Spring approaches unevenly, tossing hours of sun into strings of chilly drizzly days. Last week my back porch was bathed in warmth. I sat in my wicker chair, turned to the light, closed my eyes, felt heat. Through my eyelids, a rosy glow. I pushed up sleeves, took off socks, rolled up sweatpants, felt light and warmth paint my skin. Pores became portals. From within, a sense of being held, inside out.

It's Never Just About the Hair

My hairbrush was feathered with silver strands. Shaking, I grabbed my hair and pulled. Hair covered my palm. I got in the shower and shampooed it. Around the drain, a pale nest. I dropped the towel I used to dry my head — covered with hair — went to sit on the edge of my bed.

Our hair signals to us that body, beauty, identity, loss, change, death are on the same dance floor. Hair grows from our body, visibly changes over time and is part of relationships embedded in stories of who we are.

When people respond to another's hair or lack of it, it's never simple.

My oncologist had said specifically, "Here's the good news: you won't lose your hair this time. Different drugs." I brightened. Going bald two years ago during chemotherapy had been grim. It took eight months for my hair to grow out enough that people's eyes didn't stare at my head a bit too long. Every day, I missed my hair: texture, colour, style, image in the mirror.

As drugs turned me puffy, took lustre from my eyes and killed my hair, I took a photo during each chemo appointment. La-Z-Boy. Pillows. IV tubing. Exposed head. I took pictures because I needed proof of what was happening to me. Often I said aloud, "I'm glad Mom isn't alive to witness this." The images live unseen in my iPhone.

As long as I knew her, my mom was curiously but definitively focused on hair — her own and everyone else's. None of her four daughters escaped her comments on hair style or colour. By the time we were teenagers, we all were sick to death of her critique.

When we were girls, Mom had us all in braids. Tine of comb down middle part, then yank! Fast fingers created thin braids above temples and plaits that flopped down backs. The snap of rubber bands signalled the end. "Next," said Mom. I can still find the sting in my scalp.

At eleven I was tall and tubular, freckled, shy, serious about school. I made good grades, loved reading. My ashy brown hair hung below my shoulder blades, long enough for me to grasp the ends of my braids. When alone, I wrapped them around my head, imagined I was Peggy Woods from the TV show *I Remember Mama*, or loosened them into a cape to watch swing, hand mirror held high.

My hair was the only beautiful thing about me.

On the day I remember too well, I was leaning into my father's bathroom mirror, studying my hair, when a sawing sound close to my left ear made me jerk. Another sawing sound. My left braid thunked on the tile floor. Behind me in the mirror, my older sister Nancy, eyes wild. "I *told* you not to wear my clothes." Hair on the left side flopped forward.

I grabbed it. "*Mom! Mom! Mom!*"

Up the back stairs, Mom's feet stomped.

"What have you girls done now?" Her eyes dropped to the floor. Her hand covered her mouth.

Nancy placed shears on the back of the toilet and walked out. I sobbed. Mom put her arms around me. Nancy and I didn't speak to one another about it.

Not long after the braid disaster, Mom went to New York to be "permed" at Elizabeth Arden; she returned enthused about "permanent waves."

Newly popular was Toni's permanent-wave home kit. Nancy and I were hesitant, but we went along with Mom's plans to make everything easier. While we read directions, she wound hair onto pink plastic spools, poured horrid-smelling liquids over our heads, set a timer, poured more awful stuff over us, pulled out spools, and told us to bend over so she could rinse.

In the mirror: frizz, kinks, red welts, wayward corkscrews. How to style that was a mystery. Thankfully, friends at school also had moms enthused about home perms who had no idea what to do next. There are a lot of chopped fuzzy girls in my grade-five and -six class pictures. Nancy and I have agreed we never looked as hideous as during the "Toni years," which thankfully were few.

When we became teenagers, we chose our own hairstyles. I headed toward June Allison and Rosemary Clooney, turned my now-blond hair into a pageboy, shining with just the right amount of DuSharme. When Peter, Paul and Mary came along, I parted my hair on the side and wore it straight as linguini. On dates, I became Julie London — hair wound into a chignon, piled high, or woven and clamped down with hairspray.

When my sons were teens, they scoffed at my tidy ideas for their hair, grew their hair into braids, wound it into topknots, fuzzed it into dreadlocks, buzzed it to a bristle. I watched, horrified, curious, envious. I tried to say little.

During a visit from Mom, my older son teased his long blond hair into a wild bush and sat down at the dining room table next to his grandmother. Her eyes went wide. Her jaw dropped. "Oh my God," she squeaked.

Until she was too close to death to sit up for several hours, my mom had perms. After the mid-1950s, she settled into a style she replicated for decades: above the collar, swept back in anxious waves. Once a week she took her "do" to her hairdresser — a regular wash, set, comb-out, spray. When she had a perm she fussed, "It'll calm down." My sisters and I tried for years to entice her into a new style.

Weeks before she died, so weak she could barely sit up, Mom asked me to take her to her hairdresser. I held her too-thin arm to help her climb into the chair. I watched her jaundiced face and closed eyes as her hair was tended by a woman Mom had known for decades.

My chest clamped. Tears. I closed my eyes.

I knew Mom figured out her emotions by judging how she looked on the outside, that her hair even influenced attitudes toward others. This appointment was deeply important. As long as her mirror reflected a style she could pat into familiar waves, she knew who she was.

Soon after that appointment, my sisters and I sought a palliative care volunteer who "knew hair" and found Dottie, a retired schoolteacher who understood women who wanted to die with elegance. She came, talked to Mom about her hair, then washed and styled it to perfection. Mom relished her touch. Dottie offered a pleasure her daughters couldn't provide. What we could do was brush her hair. Nancy, Casey, Suzie and I took turns, her back against our legs, brushing in silence, an act that tossed me back to childhood, when snow fell so thick no one went out. Kids played board games, Dad and Mom read. While she read, I brushed my mom's hair.

What was it with Mom and hair? Her own mom hadn't been hands-on, probably never washed or styled her three daughters' hair. Maybe it was Kittie, a live-in governess, German, who never cut her own hair but spent hours braiding her long tresses. She must have washed, waved, listened to girlish thoughts. How did she teach them the language of hair? Was hair a hobby? Art? Link to home country?

I was fascinated by Kittie's braids: silky, shiny, tawny then silver, wound around her head like a nest of exotic snakes. When I was nine, I found one of her hairpins, an ivory U-shaped wiggle. I held it to my nose, inhaled deeply. Body scent. Kittie's. Part of her private ablutions. I pulled my braids around my head and poked the hairpin in, but they flopped down. How did she do it? I planned to grow my hair to my knees, like Kittie's.

When I was twenty-two, I remembered the lost hairpin. I was visiting my widowed grandfather, who shared his house with a now very old Kittie. They were like ancient puppets, creaking their way from one meal to the next. I knocked on Kittie's door. When she opened it, I gasped. Hanging off her head — six braids that reached to her knees. Gleaming ribbons. She patted the bed. Her fingers, like nimble spiders, unbraided the plaits.

"May I brush it for you, Kittie?"

She handed me the brush. I pulled it crown-to-end through this elegant antiquated fabric, ran fingers through waves, separated tangles, felt silky strands on my skin, breathed in. Kittie's scent.

"How do you want me to leave your hair for you?"

"One long braid, no rubber band. It knows what to do."

I divided her hair three ways, wove, then settled her beneath covers, the white braid on the top, a ceremonial serpent.

"Thank you . . . so much." Eyes closed. Sleep. I knew I would never see her again.

When I was a young researcher at the University of British Columbia, by then a mom, I received a grant to study family reactions to the diagnosis and treatment for life-threatening cancer. I plumbed the kaleidoscopic shifts of life when a woman undergoes surgery, chemotherapy, radiation. I interviewed them and their families before and after surgery, several times.

While I had a strong understanding of families, I'd not explored the intimate spaces cancer touches. I needed to hear diagnoses delivered, see amputated breasts and bald heads, hear families talk. I sat in examining rooms; accompanied women to operating rooms; watched breasts or uteri get plunked into stainless steel bowls; sat in waiting rooms with husbands, children and parents; talked with whole families. When a recurrence happened, I asked about life *now*.

No one mentioned hair loss in family interviews. During one-on-one conversations, however, women talked about their hair falling to the floor, wigs put on so husbands didn't have to make love with a bald wife, a sense of relief among other bald women in a chemo room. Tears ran down cheeks. They told me they winced when friends suggested turbans and hats. Although some were unfazed by changes in hair, most claimed they were astonished to discover the importance of their hair.

I heard their words, nodded, believed I understood.

I thought their stories inoculated me: *I* couldn't get cancer, lose *my* hair.

Those stories, they were my primer.

Not long after my cancer diagnosis at seventy, I sat with eight women around a U-shaped table, all recently in treatment, referred to this session to help us cope with changes up ahead. Facilitators stood nearby. Except for a South Asian woman in a turban sitting across from me, everyone had hair.

In front of each woman, makeup, cotton pads and makeup remover, provided by cosmetics companies. Wigs sat perkily on Styrofoam heads near the facilitators, who taught first why caution with germs was important. Then, beauty: how to create eyebrows and eyelashes, use products to appear healthy. Women painted faces, tried on wigs, wrapped hair in scarves, laughed.

I couldn't. Neither could the woman in the turban. I wanted to yell, but I knew if I revealed what my research subjects had taught me, it would prick a carefully inflated balloon. It wasn't my job to be a truth-teller.

Like most whose appearance is altered by treatment, I put myself together carefully, arranged skimpy hair, scarves and hats precisely. My baldness, puffiness and paleness drew attention. I wanted to *not see* the look-then-look-away when people registered *something's wrong with her.* I only wore a wig twice: to have my passport picture taken and to have my driver's license renewed. It amused me that for these photos, I *had* to have hair.

I stared at (but didn't photograph) my naked body in a large bedroom mirror. Bald head, no eyebrows or eyelashes, hairless armpits, legs, arms, pubis. Smooth and uncomplicated as a butternut squash.

I was used to being critiqued; my mom's focus on hair gave me history.

When I'd visited my mom, first her eyes zeroed in on my hair. I closed my eyes, waited.

"Oh, you've cut your hair. It looked more feminine before."

Every visit included talk of hair. Mom could determine more from a woman's hairstyle than a therapist could in months of treatment. I came to think about Mom's hair behaviour as similar to those who depend on astrology to determine character, intent, mood.

During the 1970s, an enthusiastic feminist, I pared down, relinquished whatever grabbed men's attention, suggested I was a sex object. I reclaimed my natural hair colour, cut long tresses short, stopped wearing makeup and jewellery. My husband wept. He'd loved my blond hair more than anything else about me, he said.

Along with my mom, he fretted: What Is Happening with her hair?

During the 1980s, asymmetrical haircuts and splashes of colour became popular. Turning forty and feeling spunky, husband gone, I had the left side cut short and the longer right side dyed fuchsia and green.

On a visit to Mom's, I felt her eyes before I saw her at the airport. For the next week I would be with her, accompany her and my stepfather to parties hosted by couples Mom had known for decades. I liked her friends and they liked me.

"Now *why* would you do *that* to your hair?" Her arms straight at her sides.

I hugged her. "Hi Mom." Then, "It's *hair*, Mom. It's to play with. It grows."

She shrugged, shook her head.

That evening, we drank white wine, her dogs nearby, her husband asleep.

"I need to cancel the party we were going to give you."

I said nothing. Then, "Your call, Mom. But – trust your friends. Tell them you think I look like a freak. Maybe they agree. But it will give you something to talk about."

Silence.

During the party, several guests touched my pink stripes, whispered they wished they'd "done something like that" when they were younger.

I asked Mom if she'd lost friends. Her mouth a line: "No."

Many years after Nancy cut off my braid, she gave me a box tied with a wide red satin ribbon. Inside, a yard-long braid. Although we'd often talked about the importance of hair and laughed at Mom's never-changing hairstyle, we'd not talked about the braid incident.

But then we both experienced chemotherapy and baldness. We spent hours talking about hair.

As I held the box, she asked me to forgive her for cutting my braid off.

"Of course." I felt a new depth of knowing pass between us.

"It's never just about hair, is it?" she said.

"No. I don't think so."

Grownupedness

Through whose eyes is maturity determined? Perhaps we can only understand how maturity lives within relationships when we consider when and how it evolves, who notices, and what difference it makes when they do. Grownupedness is complex, like a prism.

I have spent my life as a daughter, sibling, wife, mother, teacher, therapist. Each has provided a unique angle from which to learn how grownupedness evolves and changes over time. When I began studying and working with mid-life children and aging parents, I was a young mid-life woman with teenaged children; my mother was a perky, healthy sixty-something. By the time she died at almost ninety, I'd become an elder myself; my kids had families of their own; I was a grandmother, and an experienced therapist. My initial fascination with how parents' aging rearranges the lives of their children had morphed into a fascination with how time and aging affects everyone in the family.

My clients – mid-life children and aging parents – were always superb teachers. Most sought help with family issues when old ways of relating didn't work anymore. The lengthy journey through aging involves numerous reasons to stumble — burdensome caregiving, coping with illness, sibling strife, money dynamics, unfinished business. Family members felt stuck, agitated — even angry — about aging-related changes, impatient to make relationships work, even if they'd not worked smoothly up until now. As they opened their lives to me, showed me their inner gears at work, I listened hard. As I took in their stories, I searched for similarities and differences among families, offered ideas about what might be going on, looked for openings to step forward.

Eventually I began to sense a pivot point around which most family issues spun. No matter what they were particularly upset about, mid-life children and old parents alike wanted to be seen as an adult, to act grown-up in front of one another. Parents' aging, especially illness, called for responsible approaches to tough situations, respect for differences in perspective, authentic and open conversation, boundaries. Relationships had to change. Maturity was needed. Grownupedness. Despite deep desire for responsible relationships, for some, the effort, time, patience and cooperation among family members it took to shift such an intimate bond was more than they wanted to do, could do. No matter how I counselled, I was unsuccessful in helping them let go of old patterns and risk new ones. For others, risks taken paid off; connections shifted.

This work traces when and how grownupedness emerges and evolves, what threatens or cobbles it together; what it looks and sounds like in action over time. I draw on stories of my own growing pains and successes, and the stories of clients — all of us after the same sense of sharing respected space and voice within our most important relationships.

When I turned seventy, I asked for a week with just my sons, who were then forty-five and forty-three. No daughters-in-law. No grandchildren. My idea of a perfect marker for this birthday was simplicity, intimacy, uninterrupted conversations, a firm respect for the unique intensity so often characteristic of single-parent families. That had certainly been true in ours. The three of us would go someplace we'd never been and celebrate ourselves. It would be our "Three Bears Retreat."

We met in Quebec City, where I'd rented a large top-floor suite at the Hotel Frontenac. My younger son Larson, making good use of his years of French immersion, was able to get us checked in and oriented to the massive building. We made up each day a few hours at a time: galleries, museums, breweries, amazing meals, conversation. Hours of walking, traipsing up and down the stone steps into and out of the oldest part of the city.

One night over dinner in a quiet dimly-lit restaurant — wood and leather furniture — I told them I wanted their attention. They stopped mid-sentence and went silent.

I'd thought about this moment for weeks.

"I need you to listen to me for a while, then I want to hear your thoughts and suggestions, concerns."

Then I opened a conversation about my future and their involvement in it: finances, caregiving, their juggling their own families and parts of my life if and when I became ill. I told them I wanted them both to hold power of attorney and to be health representatives, that I'd planned for my future financially, so they didn't need to worry I'd tap into theirs. That they both lived geographically distant presented a particular dilemma.

"I don't expect you to leave your lives except for visits, as you've been doing. And crises." We all laughed. "Should I collapse, I'll arrange for outsiders to do any intimate care necessary; that's not how I want us to spend our time together."

"What if I feel okay doing that?" asked Chandler.

"Bless you, but I'd rather you hold my hand than wipe my ass."

"Oh, *that* kind of personal care."

"Yeah."

"Good to know," Larson said.

"I want to stay in my own home unless it becomes impossible." They nodded. "And I want you with me when I die."

Chandler let out a puff of air. Larson looked at the ceiling, then me, then the ceiling.

The conversation went on for a couple of hours over seafood, craft beer and breaks from the seriousness of it to laugh. We kept talking; I knew these conversations had to happen.

Chandler tossed his long arm around my shoulders. "Okay, I think I got it. You, Larson?"

"Yup. Got it. You okay, Mother?"

"Ready to stop talking about this and to head for the lounge at the Frontenac, where you can barter with the waiter for the perfect martini."

That night, I felt like a grown-up mother. I knew I'd invited them into a world where they, too, would be expected to be very grown-up. I'd done a great deal of thinking about what the rest of my life might look like, and now I was pushing them to think about how it might affect them — a grown-up thing to ponder.

That night in Quebec City, it would have been preposterous to imagine that within six months my children would learn their mother had late-stage cancer and faced surgery and months of chemotherapy.

When the pain in my upper abdomen wouldn't go away, I called Chandler, who happened to be working in Vancouver. "I need to go to the emergency room. Can you take me?"

It was several months after our week in Quebec.

Moments later he was at my house, his eyes dark with worry. *His* mother didn't have emergencies. We drove to the closest hospital, where he held me upright as I told the receptionist about my pain, which sliced into me more than anything physical I'd ever felt. Within minutes I was lying on a table in a small stark room, my body folded around the pain. A nurse started an IV drip of morphine in my right arm. It did little to unwind the pain. More morphine squirted into the tube.

Chandler sat nearby on the floor, knees bunched up, head in his hands, eyes trained on the nurse, my face, the nurse. As much as I wanted to, I couldn't comfort him; I couldn't even comfort myself. My eyes seemed to be looking inwards, into a place I didn't know anything about. Every few minutes Chandler got up, stroked my head, moved my hair out of my eyes, told me everything would be okay, we'd figure it out. Then he called his brother. My ears held their murmurs.

Two days later, we three sat in my downstairs suite where they were staying. We stared at one other. I was no longer in pain, had been scheduled for a rush CT scan. I'd sat with a radiologist, who delivered bad news. By the time Larson arrived from Boston, he'd researched my diagnosis, was eager to talk to the oncologist. Chandler again told the story of the emergency-room visit and what had transpired; we all needed to hear it again to believe it.

I opened a bottle of very expensive Scotch, put three of my grandfather's crystal shot glasses on the table, and pushed us to talk about the biggest crisis to visit us since I'd become a single parent forty-three years before. Tomorrow we would meet with the oncologist, who would lay out treatment options. After that: visits to my lawyer, accountant and financial advisor, where we would discuss power of attorney, health representative, executorships, taxes.

But that night we sipped Scotch, talked about my dismal prognosis and what it meant to all of us. Cried. Laughed. Cried more when I listed all the family events I did *not* want to miss and most likely would. It was an extraordinary evening. I got drunk, watched tears fall from my sons' eyes and felt a fierce love toward them.

Over the next few days, as we spoke with family, the lawyer, the accountant, I saw two men who leaned forward, made eye contact, asked these professionals hard questions, asked me what I wanted and how I felt. Someone had my back. My *sons* were embracing my vulnerability and figuring out what their responsibilities were.

Rarely had I felt so sure someone would catch me if I fell over.

When I was younger than my children are now, my research and clinical practice weren't focused on how mid-life children and their old parents matured, but on mid-life women. My interest in aging began when I read results of my research at the time on multiple-role women — those employed, married or partnered, raising children, and working known high-stress jobs. During the 1980s, the lives of women trying to "have it all" drew attention. Funding was available to study them. My interest led to collecting data from groups of women about sources of and responses to stress in their lives.

As expected, for most the interface between home and work responsibilities was troublesome. Specifically, however — and this is what grabbed my fascination — women described in detail the stress of caring for elderly parents while trying to manage the rest of their lives. They described their parents' health issues and the resultant responsibilities that fell into their lives. For years. Many were convinced that their *own* current health struggles were related to the particular burden of caring for their aging parents for a long time. Mother or Dad had been the first patient; now they were the second.

Not so long ago, I knew, the lifespans of such parents had been shorter, their daughters less likely to be in the workforce. Now oldsters' longevity was stretched by enriched lifestyles and more sophisticated health care. Their time of being old, frail, living with chronic illness was expanding, and with it, their care needs. That's what the mid-life daughters were detailing. *No one seems to care about what it's like to have kids*, a job, old sick parents — all at once, they wrote. I decided to reorient my research and clinical practice, aim both toward these troubled daughters.

I wanted to see if there were ways to head upstream, defuse stress before it blossomed into illness.

A client I met soon after I refocused my clinical practice was an employed mid-life daughter who lived with and cared for two frail parents and her own single-parent daughter, who struggled to stay employed. For years the client had juggled job, parent care and grandparenting. When I met her she was exhausted, had serious health issues and a lot to say about how burden infuses the body and psyche. "It's like wrestling an ever-bigger dragon," she said to me. "It gets you in the end."

Although I met with the whole family several times, I was unsuccessful in initiating a shift in dynamics quickly enough to protect the daughter from overextending and threatening her own health. Such changes take time and patience. Her health issues worsened until *she* became the most vulnerable member of the family. She exemplified my most serious worries about mid-life women. And she fanned my desire to figure out what behaviour families needed to exhibit for the journey through aging to work well — in other words, no one goes down with the ship.

———————————

It's 1994: in front of me is a large circle of mid-life daughters and sons, sitting in chairs with arms, backs and padded seats, all there to discuss the intricacies of relationships with aging parents.

"What does it take — in your family — to be seen as a grown up *by your parents*?" I ask.

People stare at me.

"I'll start. For my parents, we — my brothers, sisters and I — had to live away from home, be married, have children, and — for my father — be employed."

I'd never met a son or daughter who didn't want to be seen as grown-up by their parents. Or an older parent who didn't want to be treated like a grown-up by their son or daughter. Everyone in that room had been touched by parents' aging. Many were involved in caregiving. They wanted to talk about these changes. Most already knew they'd likely spend at least ten or more years engaged in parents' lives in ways they'd never anticipated.

As I stood in front of the group, I realized my own children were now the age I was when I began to work with families experiencing the bumps of aging. In the last ten years, as my mother and stepfather had aged and become frail, I'd personally experienced how one generation's aging and maturing touches another's, like interlocking gears designed to carry the family into its own future.

A voice: "In my family, too, you have to be married. And employed." Others nod.

"Yeah, in mine, it's having kids."

"In mine, it's a university degree. And owning a house."

"Financially independent."

"*Not* living with parents!"

I move on. "So for some of us, geographic and financial independence and having a family are important. What about *emotional* independence?"

Eyes drop.

"Well, *that* hasn't happened yet!" Heads nod.

"What needs to happen?" I ask.

"I don't know . . . Maybe they'll have to die." Uncomfortable laughter.

Silence. I wonder what is released, set free, by parents' deaths.

Somehow we all know that feeling grown-up is an essential piece of claiming and unfurling one's own life story. Grownupedness opens the way to maturity — the ability to make decisions, carry a load, appreciate others' perspectives, exercise opinions that represent a personal point of view even when others disagree.

For all of us, adolescence and young adulthood can be *the* times to "individuate" from parents, in other words, to piece together a unique identity, practise being our own person. Rebellious, reactive behaviours are often our portals to grownupedness, which lead to emotional separateness. Children express personal values and take steps into their own life course, and parents do the best they can to hear children's pleas and make room for new expectations.

I turn toward the group. "What about the first time you said no to your parents, meant it, and they Got It?"

Stories pour out: a defiant choice of girlfriend or boyfriend, decision to let go of a sport parents counted on, drop out of school, go to a university parents disapproved of, take a year off, costume oneself in ways parents couldn't understand. Some encounters simmered, silent standoffs. Others sparked, reactive noisy showdowns.

"It took about a year to tell Mother and Dad, *over and over*, that I was *not* ready for more school. I wanted to travel. It was exhausting. Eventually they said, 'Well, okay. It's your life. We have to trust you.' Something shifted that day. I felt . . . respected, more grown-up."

Others shake their heads. "I never rebelled. I moved out, got a job, married. But something else needed to happen. Still does. When is it too late to feel grown-up around parents? I don't want to be at my parents' funerals realizing it took their death for me to grow up."

"There are many kicks at this can," I say. "Adolescence is just a beginning. Maturing and aging present numerous opportunities for children — and their parents — to grow up a bit more." I pause. "I think it takes conflict, rich conversations, risking change . . . and a lot of practice."

"What are some of those 'kicks at the can'?"

"You may, for example, refuse to get in the car with a parent you know is not competent to drive. Or refuse to take sides in a family squabble. Or refuse to participate in unethical or illegal activities for a parent."

Nodding heads.

"As our parents age, and — usually — eventually become frail, their need for assistance from you or your siblings jostles connections in the family. They're not who they were when they were younger. And neither are you. Growing up and older reconfigures boundaries, topics of conversation, time spent together. Think about it: as your family landscape changes, you need to be as clear as possible about how you spend time, physical space, money, heart on your parents and siblings. Each of these — time, space, money, emotional support — offers opportunities to grow up a bit more. You'll want to teach your parents how much of you is available, and they need to teach you what they do and don't want from you. This happens in conversations about delicate stuff, hard-to-talk-about topics; that's how appropriate boundaries are established. Too little conversation means we're out of date, operating on never-discussed assumptions. This causes misunderstandings and conflict. If you don't know what your parents expect of you for the next twenty years, this is a good time to open that conversation."

Everyone has a story about their trek to become an adult. Sometimes children initiate shifts in connection with parents. Sometimes parents do. Sometimes exterior events force us to grow up whether we want to or not.

I left childhood behind the year I was ten, when my sister was born and died. That same year my father had a near-fatal heart attack that ended his career, and my maternal grandmother almost died of a heart attack. My family fell apart. Fearful I would lose her too, I held on to my mother, who held on to me. She showed me adult grief. I learned to listen, hold another's heart, not be a source of trouble. Terrible things *do* happen to good people. My mother taught me how to prop people up.

Five years later my father's left leg clotted and became gangrenous. There was talk of amputation. Numbed by morphine, afraid of dying, he held my fifteen-year-old hand, told me I was a comforting presence in his hospital room, talked to me about death, suicide, topics no one had ever mentioned to me before. After his amputation he sought my reassurance and presence and I offered it. The time I spent with him taught me that children can become grown-up even when they shouldn't yet.

I was a serious, independent, wary teenager. A straight-A student. Active in student politics. I knew, because they told me, I was the one child out of my parents' eight they believed they didn't have to worry about. They trusted my judgment. With everything.

The "other me" hid behind closed doors, stole their liquor and sipped bourbon and 7 Up, wrote sexual poetry late into the night. She crept out the window to meet a boyfriend at midnight. She ached for Mother and Dad's attention.

On the verge of being sexually active, I stormed into my parents' room very late one night, said, "Wake up!" Both sat up in bed, their faces scrunched with worry.

"I need a curfew."

"Not you! You are so . . . responsible. We don't worry about you!"

"*Worry* about me. Please. I need a curfew or I will get pregnant."

"Be home by 10:30," said my father.

"Thank you."

Perhaps it was the most loving thing he ever said to me.

Now, I realize I chased my parents into being adult enough to encourage my own growing up.

A more recent growing-up moment happened not long ago, during a visit to my older sister Nancy during the final weeks of her life. She and I had talked about what would happen during my days with her; this visit was to be a one-on-one goodbye time.

Hours after my flight arrived, I was huddled on a bed in Nancy's guest room, sobbing into a pillow and saying, "No, no, no . . ." My stability was fraying. I needed to talk to someone. Someone who knew Nancy. Who knew me. Who knew we were raised as two peas in a pod. Who "got" my sense of devastation that I'd come all this way, knew it was the last time I'd see her, understood why I needed quiet time and space to be with her, not what was happening all around me.

Although I rarely reached out to my sons when I felt distraught, when I did I usually turned to Larson, a philosophical physicist, deeply spiritual, to offer words that calmed me. I knew how tied up he'd be at work. Couldn't call him. Exchanges with Chandler about feelings usually happened over beer and hamburgers, not on the phone. My two other sisters were immersed in work, wouldn't pick up at 3:00 p.m.

Chandler was self-employed. More interruptible. He picked up on the first ring. "Hi, Mama."

"I'm falling apart. Unravelling. What am I doing here? It's awful. There's people everywhere, Nancy's chorus friends, your cousin. My sister wanted to go *shopping*, for fuck's sake, so we spent time going store to store after I arrived. I feel like shit. You know what travel does to me – it makes me *sick*. I came all this way because she begged me to come so we could sit and talk, say goodbye. And it's a . . . fucking *zoo*! I want to go home. I can't stand this. This is the last time I'll see her. Doesn't she *get that*? That's not gonna happen — this . . . *circus* . . . is gonna happen."

Born one year after the other, Nancy and I had been one another's confidantes for decades. Since she became ill fifteen years ago, I have flown to Oregon to visit frequently. When she was well enough, she came to Vancouver. We travelled together. After I was diagnosed with cancer a few years ago, our get-togethers were coordinated with my treatments. During the last year — a time of surgery and pain control for her and side effects from chemo for me — I visited three times. But we talked over the miles almost daily, at night, both of us in bed, our voices soft and sisterly.

From Chandler, silence on the phone.

Then, my son's soft bass voice: "Mother, if I were in your shoes I'd feel the same way you do: angry and devastated."

I stopped crying.

I was not alone.

"Thank you."

"Hey, that was pretty good wasn't it? You asked for help and I said the right thing."

"Yes, you did."

"You taught me well, Mother."

I felt the gears of growing up turn. For both of us.

In my memory, times my children and I have lurched forward into our maturity are captured in scenes, moments that live on because what happened seized my wonder and changed my understanding of them and me.

Three years before I became a grandmother, a growing-up moment happened with my twenty-nine-year-old son Chandler and his wife Angela. They had driven to Vancouver from the Kootenays for a Christmas week filled with family events: meals and movies that included my ex-husband's family, Angela's father, many of Chandler and Angela's friends. I'd known most of their friends since they were in primary school and loved watching them mature. Many evenings were filled with laughter, beer-drinking, music, stories of their evolving lives. We'd agreed on a ten-day visit.

We were at day twelve.

I returned to work after New Year's, the same day my son and his wife were to travel back home. A heavy snowfall postponed their departure, and my house again filled up with their friends. As much as I enjoyed and welcomed them, we'd again said goodbye to the holidays last night, and I was ready to have my house back. I was finding the liberty taken with my family room, food and beer uncomfortable. My going off to work while others slept in and ignored dishes crowded in my kitchen sink was turning me crabby.

Five days after the snow melted, I said to Chandler and Angela, "We agreed on ten days and it's been two weeks. I need my house back. My life. I love you and your friends, but it's time for you to go."

"You're kicking us out?" Both were wide-eyed.

"Yes, I guess I am. It's been a wonderful holiday and now it's time for me to work."

Silence. They got up from the table, put their dishes in the dishwasher and went upstairs. The next morning they were gone. No goodbye.

Days later, two emails arrived at the same time. One, a rant: How could I? How dare I? They assumed . . . They'd done nothing to deserve . . . A second, dated two days after the first, said I was appropriate to draw a line in the sand — for them, for their friends. It was presumptuous for them to assume they could stay as long as they wanted, callous of them to allow their friends to treat my house as if it were their own. He apologized for taking me for granted, for being insensitive. He included the first diatribe, he said, to show me his change in thinking over several days.

"It's so easy to stay a child, Mother, taken care of and fed long beyond it's okay," he wrote.

It's been many years since those letters, but my son and his wife have never since assumed they could arrive when they want and stay as long as they please. I am always asked if it's okay for their friends to spend time at my house. Only once has Chandler asked me if the email diatribe had ruined anything.

"Not really. I kind of saw it as your farewell-to-boyhood letter. I've kept it in case you want to reread it."

This experience within my family, as do all situations that involve an invitation to grow up, involved risk-taking and decision-making about the losses and gains afoot. It's impossible to grow forward without leaving behind part of one's self, opportunities, familiarity — in other words, to experience loss. Identifying and trusting gains such as increased independence, more confidence, deeper relationships, expanded use of one's gifts, etc., can be more difficult than feeling the losses. It takes courage to grow up.

Three years after I read those emails, my first grandchild's birth happened during another relentless snowfall. Because their back-country community had no services, Chandler and Angela again came to live with me in Vancouver for six weeks over Christmas. I was happy to be able to offer this, to be such a special part of their child's arrival. They set up my upstairs guest room for a home birth. The midwife, a former student of mine, visited daily. With her help they meticulously planned a natural, no-intervention home birth,

For days labour started, stopped, started again. Then, blood pressure rose and stayed elevated.

The midwife said no go, and Angela was whisked off. Now in a hospital bed, IVs dripping, monitors beeping, an obstetrician on board, she and Chandler wept about the danger their baby was in and talked about choices. The doctor and midwife gave them as much time as was safely allowed to choose between a risky vaginal birth and a C-section. I paced, said little, though I desperately wanted to shout *get that baby out of there*. To keep me quiet I bought food, brought it to the waiting room and to the room where Angela lay in bed, her best friend and Chandler's younger brother Larson by her side.

In the waiting room, Chandler sat in a straight-backed chair, his face in his hands, shoulders shaking, tears falling to the floor. Deep moans and sighs emerged from his chest.

I wrapped my arms around him. His neck was hot, sweaty. I felt his heart thump.

"Mother, this is awful. I don't know these feelings. I've never been in a place like this before."

I knew I had to say something soothing. My son and I had had many moments of testiness, especially if he felt I wasn't respecting his life or decisions. I took a deep breath. "Oh, my dear son. You are becoming a father, Chandler. This is what it feels like."

"Oh my God. My baby is in trouble. What if . . . ?"

"Here. You've not eaten in ten hours. Eat something. It will help you. Then, go to Angela and make your decision." He stared at me, tears flowing.

I took another deep breath, hesitated and hoped, said, "I'm right behind you, sweetheart, but this is your call."

"We didn't want any of *this*." His hand swept the bland-walled room.

"What you want now is a live, healthy baby."

Inside me, a swirling sense of time, a piercing awareness of the power of this exact moment. In the background, memories of my own frighteningly similar first birth.

My son's shoulders lowered, seemed to broaden. He nodded at me, as if an initiation to fatherhood was something he could handle. He stood up, sandwich in hand, and went to his wife. Moments later the two of them were in the operating room. The rest of us waited. Finally, flushed and ebullient, dressed in green scrubs, he walked into the waiting room, a bundle of baby with an electric shock of flame hair in his arms.

"My daughter!" he exclaimed.

After that day, my son never looked or sounded the same to me. He'd become a man with deeper, broader feelings, a man whose love and consideration spread wider.

When my younger son, Larson, was thirty-five, he suggested we go out for dinner. After our pints of beer arrived, he said he wanted to talk with me about his upcoming move to the

East Coast. A year before, he'd met a woman from Boston, and the two of them had been flying back and forth across the continent ever since. They wanted to marry. Although she liked Vancouver, she made it clear she wouldn't leave her family in Boston. I knew about the upcoming move, but we'd not yet really talked about it.

"I thought we might have a conversation about our living so far apart from one another, Mother."

"Yes." I watched his face, felt my spine straighten slightly. A mist of sweat shone on his brow. He looked at his hands, then back at my face.

"You and I are so close. Are you going to be okay without either son in Vancouver?"

Close. Yes. Since his birth, when he rushed into the world after a breathtaking forty-minute labour, and for several years after had serious health issues which grabbed my attention and heart. I became watchful, protective, breastfed him into his second year and did a lot of worrying about what physicians would say. From his earliest days I believed we had similar temperaments, which seemed to make parenting both easier and more difficult than it had been with his older brother. For decades, because Larson and I treasured time to be alone, to think, I had to stop myself when I realized I believed I knew how he understood his world. Thankfully, we took time to explore our similarities and differences, something I learned was also important with his older brother.

I felt my throat tighten and took a swig of my beer. I had really hoped he would stay in Vancouver. Big sigh. "I will miss you. Of course. But I understand what you are doing; I did the same thing. When your father and I married, we left Fort Lauderdale to move to Los Angeles. Unlike you, we didn't think much about our parents' feelings, just about our own adventure."

"I don't want you to think I'm abandoning you."

"You're worried about me?"

"I guess I am."

I was surprised how my heart was galloping. In a couple of weeks I'd be on my own in a whole new way: no family nearby. My ex-husband and his new family had left Vancouver a few years before, not long after Chandler and Angela moved to the Kootenays, a ten-hour drive away. My closest sibling was in Oregon, nine hours away.

I knew what to say. In my years of counselling families, every time I helped them with a conversation like this, I rehearsed what I would and wouldn't say to my own mother, my own sons.

"Please instead try to trust me to find my way, Larson. Your job is to find your life and live it. My job as your mother is to support you in your decisions, and to believe in you. You're getting married and moving to Massachusetts because you want to, not because you want to get away from me, right?"

"Right." Larson nodded his head slowly, took a sip of beer, smiled. "Thanks, Mother."

"I'll visit. You know that about me. And I'll expect you to come home once in a while."

How I acted as a mother and grandmother would now be marked by geographic distance, planned visits, long-distance calls, rather than dropping by, casual encounters, tossed-together family meals. I had to figure out how to stay connected, respect boundaries, offer and receive help . . . from a distance and during episodic visits, which, I knew, would involve sudden gear shifts: concentrated encounters, family members pulled together around the dinner table, exposure to how time changes everyone — experiences as awkward to navigate as they had been with my own mother. Larson's 3,000-mile geographic move pushed me toward my own evolving grownupedness.

I don't know what stories represent my sons' thoughts about their trek to adulthood. I doubt they will match mine, but I don't expect them to.

Serious illness throws a monkey wrench in the gears of life's progression. The arrival of vulnerability messes around with the balance of power. Whether illness is physical or emotional, independence, dignity and authority are often reduced. A rearrangement of the self and family relationships takes weeks, months, or longer, depending on how serious the illness, how long it lasts, how much reorganization is necessary. Who steps forward to care and how is often part of an unspoken contract. It's an experience that grows up the carer in ways impossible to anticipate.

It's unlikely mid-life children can accurately predict how they will feel when their parent is changed by illness. The more obvious the vulnerability, the more likely they feel frightened, sad, worried. When it's time to exercise leadership, afraid of their own feelings, they may distance or slip into parental, even paternalistic, behaviours, well-intended but wrong. Mid-life sons and daughters who have raised children often, without awareness, offer caring more appropriate for children than a long-lived parent. How to avoid taking over and to instead protect the dignity of a parent, keep them as much as possible in the driver's seat of their own life, is often a thorny puzzle.

Unless both generations have spent time figuring out how to ask for and receive help from one another, it's a time of essential learning and rearrangement of the family Velcro. This takes time, talk, and trust. The back-and-forth helping process heightens awareness of how power is negotiated and renegotiated. Often this awareness begins innocently.

When my fiercely independent mother was in her late seventies, she began to lose her eyesight to macular degeneration. She still drove, weeded her own garden, entertained frequently, took care of her four dogs and cognitively impaired husband, cooked and did the lighter parts of housework. But her ophthalmologist had said her driving days were numbered. Her macular degeneration would get worse.

All seven of Mother's children visited her. We all felt protective of her; her life was increasingly wound around taking care of her husband. Her failing eyesight was making life increasingly complicated. Most of our efforts to secure housekeeping and gardening help failed; Mother was a terrible employer. She didn't know how to give direction, and "the help" ended up doing what they wanted, which often was not much at all.

It was clear that Mother needed help. When my sisters and I visited — often as a group of four — we noticed spills on the counters, greasy pans, clouds of dog hair in corners, dog poop in the back garden. When Mother put on her eye-shadow, she looked like she'd been playing with her older sister's makeup.

If we tried to clean counters or sweep the patio, she shouted, "Leave it! Leave it! You're here so we can have fun, not *work*. If you don't like what you see, take your glasses off." And then she grabbed the broom or rag or sponge from our hand and left the room, her mouth in a firm pout.

During one visit I noticed her fridge was a tangle of crusty dog food cans, mouldy cheese, and leftovers in open containers. While she was napping I emptied everything out, washed the shelves, tossed out what was inedible and reorganized remaining bottles, cans and containers.

"I cleaned out your fridge, Mother."

Her eyebrows lowered. "Why would you do a thing like that?"

"So you don't have to worry about it."

She yanked open the refrigerator and shook her head, "No, no, no." Her voice got louder with each word.

"I didn't throw anything out that wasn't rotten, Mother."

She began moving items around. "No, no, no." There were tears in her voice.

"What is it, Mother? I was just trying to help."

Now, tears in her eyes. A whisper: "But now I can't find anything."

I let out a big breath. "Oh dear. I'm so sorry."

How could I have missed it? My mother was learning how to be blind. She was mourning the loss of her eyesight, the ease of finding things. When dog food, containers of leftovers, cans of orange juice were in predictable places, she could find what she needed and competently feed her animals and prepare meals for her husband.

By failing to see her perspective, by cleaning out her fridge, I shone a spotlight on what she could no longer do. Her dignity, her sense of being a grown-up in her own world, was threatened. My job, I knew, was to make her life better, not worse, and I had dropped the ball.

I knew my mother had the right to live how she wished, to let her life unravel around her if she wanted. I also knew how deeply she loved a clean house and wanted to avoid being embarrassed in front of her children and friends. This was a conundrum for me and my sisters.

Over time we learned how to be sensitive, to offer help. Instead of "May I help you?" we learned to say "Is it okay if I'm part of this?" and "I'm doing my own ironing, how about if I do yours, too?" We learned to ask her to help *us* as we cooked or tidied. When she offered an adamant no, we backed off, even when it didn't make sense. Her right to say no, we learned, protected her independence, her capacity to *choose*. During her daily naps we quietly weeded, washed floors, finished laundry. We knew she noticed, but she rarely said more than "Oh, you girls, let's all go out for lunch. My treat."

How each of us asks for, receives and refuses help develops over time and becomes idiosyncratic. The "language of help" is spoken through voice tone, body movements, eye contact, mood shifts, timing; the word *help* may be not be uttered; "no thanks" may not be part of a refusal.

Married more than sixty years, my father's sister and her husband asked for and refused help from one another by shifting their eyebrows around.

For some, uttering, "I need help" leaves them feeling too naked, exposed. Instead, oblique references to "good days," "bad days," "I've been better," or gestures hint at their needs. Once frailty-related helping is part of the family mosaic, it becomes important to translate signals so family members speak the same language. The clearer old parents and their mid-life children are about how to interpret cues, the more likely this most human exchange will become part of relationships. Conversations that foster this nudge people to grow up.

Because exposure of needs rearranges how children and parents relate, it is the crucible in which grownupedness occurs. All family members can inch forward when needing, seeking or offering help. This potential to grow exists in all family relationships.

Rena, a married mother of two in her mid-fifties, an only child of her recently widowed eighty-two-year-old father Peter, became his primary support after her mother died. When she visited during the first month after her mother's death, it became clear her father expected her to take over domestic activities previously carried out by his wife. Rena was angry. "Dad! I have to drive fifty miles twice a week to help you out. I have two teenagers and a husband and a job! I'm not Mother. I'll do a bit of cooking, play music with you and take you on a few errands, but I'm not doing your housework."

"Who will do it?"

"Either you will, or you could hire someone."

He nodded, his brow furrowed.

Six months later, she came to see me because she was furious and discouraged. Although her dad respected her limits on what she would do, he never said "thank you" or expressed any appreciation.

"I'm not unwilling, believe me. I love my dad, but he was *so* pampered by Mother — she did everything! I'm *not* going to be his wife! And I'm *not* the hired help. I'm his *daughter*. And I will happily drive back and forth to fix him meals twice a week, play viola with him, take him out wherever he wants to go — all things I've done for years. I know he's lonely. Mother was his everything. Including his appreciation. *She* was the one who always said, 'Thanks, honey, for all you do.' " Her face went dark. Tears. "Without . . . those *words* . . . I feel like a widget in his life."

When my stepfather was in his eighties, I too felt like a widget in his life when he sought my help and I offered it. His response: silence. Like Rena's mother, appreciation came from my mother. When I told my stepfather it would be easier, and make me much happier, if he thanked me once in a while, he scowled and said, "It's your job."

When Rena and Peter and I got together, she told him about her unhappiness with his lack of appreciation. He was clearly surprised. "Isn't helping your dad part of being a daughter?"

She stared at him then dropped her eyes and fiddled with her thumbs. Her voice soft: "Not this daughter. Dad, I don't need great accolades, but I need you to . . . notice, not take me for granted. It makes me feel . . . used." Tears ran down her face. He reached over to touch her arm.

How critical the expression of appreciation for help received in our families is. How emotionally expensive the absence of "thank you" is. The words "I appreciate all you're doing," can, however, draw attention to independence lost, frailty, powerlessness, need. It can be hard to recognize that appreciation is emotional fuel for graceful giving and receiving, that gratitude fosters adult-to-adult relationships. Without appreciation, connections become brittle and snap. Understanding why a family member fails to give thanks is necessary for changing the patterns of giving and receiving.

When I asked Peter about his experience with older parents, he said he was in Canada and they were in Europe. "My sister was the one to do it. She was the daughter. I visited."

"So what Rena is experiencing, you never did. It was expected of your sister and she did the caring, right?"

"Yes, I guess so. Is that *wrong*?"

"Not necessarily. Families have all sorts of ways of working out who takes care when the time comes. I wonder, did you ever thank your sister for all she did?"

He looked startled, embarrassed. "No. Isn't it just . . . what's expected in a family?"

"Perhaps, but I'm going to try to convince you of the importance of appreciating help from others."

"Huh."

"Is it too late? To thank your sister?"

His eyes looked down. "No, she's still alive and we talk on the phone every few weeks." He looked at Rena.

"And what about you, Peter? What do you need to be thanked for?"

"Me?" He put his chin in his hands, looked back at his daughter. "All I did to make our life in Canada happen, I guess. My work."

"And . . ."

"Rena thanked me often for all I've done."

"I don't need much appreciation from you, Dad, for the cooking and errands: 'thanks,' a hug, a kiss. I'm not that hard to please."

Peter turned to me. "You ever have this trouble in your family?"

"Yes. With my stepfather. He was a vet, World War II. He told me in war there's no time to say thanks. I helped him with health issues and with his books, and wanted my time and effort noticed — and told him so. Like your wife, my mother did the thanking." Peter nodded. "I had to hold my ground. I wanted to be treated like an adult by him and knew, like Rena does, that being clear about what I needed and setting limits is part of that. He never got comfortable expressing thanks verbally, but he began to nod and sometimes sort of cough and grunt his appreciation. What I felt was new respect for me. After a while, we got along better."

"You stood up to him." Peter looked me straight on.

"Yes. I wanted us to know one another as adults, to be able to say no to one another. To respect one another's experience."

"Huh."

Most old parents, as soon as they need to depend on relatives for help, worry about being a burden. The longer reliance goes on, especially if "giving back" is difficult, the more they ponder whether they have become a heavy load, an interruption, a drag. Relatives involved in helping often feel burdened, especially after energy and time spent goes on for years. Concerns are often borne silently, words hard to find. What isn't hard to find are *feelings* about burden: hollowed out inside, exhausted, no more lightness, heavy shoulders. The sense of burden sticks to everything. By the time loved ones talk to one another about this, specifics about caring may have become hard to describe and thus to change.

Rose sits examining her nails. Across the room sit Sandra and Caroline, her two daughters, both in their mid-sixties. Rose is ninety-one. This family has been coming for counselling sessions off and on for two years. It was Rose who suggested the family find a counsellor who "wasn't afraid of old people" to help them talk about her health changes.

"I'm a burden," Rose blurts out.

Both daughters turn toward their mother. "Oh, Mother, don't be silly," says Sandra.

"Really, Mother," adds Caroline.

"Sure I am. You don't have to be afraid to tell me the truth. I can take it."

"I'm not lying, Mother," retorts Caroline angrily.

I hold up my hand. "Wait a minute. This is going too fast for me. Okay if I slow it down a bit?"

Rose looks back at her lap.

"Can we start at the beginning? Tell me, what does this word *burden* mean to you? To each of you? Rose?"

"It's awful being this old. I've lived too long. No one wants to take care of an old lady who can't see or hear, who rushes to the bathroom, who needs help to do stairs."

"Is that what you mean by *burden*?"

"I guess. I don't know." I know Rose likes good questions and I can see she likes this one. She adjusts her glasses. "A person is a burden when they've become someone you don't want to care for, when you feel put upon, when it's just . . . too much, *too hard*."

"What makes someone burdensome, Rose?"

Rose looks intently at me, then her daughters. She purses her lips. "When they're selfish. When they complain. And they're negative. Glass half-empty, you know the type. I'll bet you see a lot of us." She laughs, adds quietly, "People like me."

"What happens to people who are a burden?"

"Their children don't like them, want to get rid of them."

"Do you think your daughters find you selfish, negative, complaining?"

"I don't know. Maybe."

"Do you want to know what they think?"

"I don't want them to send me away."

"What would you do if you thought you were a burden to your children?"

"I don't know."

I ask the daughters what they think *burden* is.

"*Burden* sounds so . . . unwelcoming, so judgmental." Sandra looks at Caroline. "We're doing what we want to do. We've figured out ways to get Mother to the bathroom, to help her get out and about as much as possible."

"So those things aren't burdensome." Both daughters shake their heads no. "If you started to feel burdened by caring for your mother, what would cause that? And what would you do?"

Rose sits forward, cups her hand around her ear.

"I'd tell you to shape up, Mother," says Caroline, "to stop being such a drag!"

Sandra puts her hand on her mother's shoulder. "We won't send you away, Mother, because you're . . . having a bad hair day and have a lot to say about it. Promise. If you had to go in care, it would be because you said you wanted to or we couldn't figure this out any other way."

"You mean I complain a lot, don't I?" says Rose to her daughters.

Sandra jumps in. "Yes. Especially when you don't feel well. Or need help."

I turn toward Rose. "Is complaining a signal for 'I need help'?"

Rose nods.

Caroline's eyes spark with anger. "You want to work on something, Mother? Work on that! I'd rather have you ring a bell or write me a note or just yell 'Help' than complain about everything from the weather to your friends to your apartment. *That* I find burdensome. *You're* not a burden, but the complaining drives me nuts."

The specificity in Caroline's retort sits in the middle of the room. Silence. Rose stares at her daughter.

"Rose, what do you want from your daughters?"

"What she just did! Tell me! I don't even know when I do it. Being all old and wobbly is hard for me. I can't do anything about that. And . . . I know you can't either. But I can try to stop being a 'drag'!" She nods.

"Here's what I like about your idea, Rose," I say. "You want your daughters to *tell* you if you're doing something that is turning you into someone they don't like. And you're willing to work on setting boundaries around complaining. It takes time to *become* a burden or to *feel burdened*, and it's no one complaint or selfish act that will create it. Burden develops over time, kind of like plaque does on teeth. Burden is like emotional plaque. It builds up when we expect more than can be given from our loved ones. When there's too little appreciation for help, or not enough delegating of responsibility, not enough time to replenish when caring goes on for a while. My guess is, you'd like to count on your daughters to protect themselves from feeling burdened, and count on yourself to pay attention to what makes you 'a drag.' Your hip fracture changed the way the three of you related to one another. You saw and heard one another more, were more exposed to each other's ways of doing things. You've done a good job getting your hip going. Recently, you've rejoined activities: church friends, walking partners, writing. Now more than ever, all of that is important for you, Rose — and for you, Caroline and Sandra. Making sure there is complexity in your life prevents caring from swamping your connections with one another, from creating a sense of burden."

"This is like going to boundary school, isn't it?" says Caroline.

"Something like that."

By the time illness or frailty turns a mid-life child toward their old mother or father, there is a long history of attachment between parent and child. Throughout the length of a relationship that begins before birth, the shape and feel of this bonding shifts with the twists and turns of life. Healthy relationships begin with a close intense intimacy between infant and parent; this is essential — literally — to keep a baby alive. This type of bond loosens as a child stands, talks, connects with other children, discovers she, her mother and father are separate people. Ideally, parents allow room for this healthy development, in other words, say fond goodbyes to the earlier child and hello to their ever-evolving, more independent child. It's tricky: too much physical and emotional space creates fear, not delight; too little suppresses the air needed to blow a sense of self into the child. There are many reasons why early bonding might get off to a bumpy start and leave shadows that are hard to lighten thereafter.

Pulled ever forward by constantly changing bodies and life experiences, children and their parents are faced with getting to know who they *now* are, to let go of who they just were weeks or months ago. As newness arrives and

Grownupedness

takes up space, it jostles the stuff out of which a connection with another is made. In order to now fit with one another, the elements that moderate closeness, intimacy, and getting along need to adjust. Because it takes time and acknowledgment to rework bonding, children and their parents are often out of date with one another.

I first met fifty-seven-year-old Roy, an owner of a small IT company 500 miles away from Vancouver, because his sister Louise insisted he "see someone." She was exasperated, she said on the phone, because her older brother didn't want to spend time with their mother or father when he visited. He just wanted to "go over the books" during his monthly visits. Because their dad had dementia and Mother didn't, Roy and Louise's parents were in different facilities. Louise tried to visit each twice a week.

"I need some company on this journey!" she said. "He promised he'd see you next time he came to Vancouver if I set it up. I don't want to be there. Okay?" I agreed, as long as she would agree to come with him at some point.

I met with Roy on his own several times. He hoped his seeing me would allow his sister to see him as useful, a good brother. She was a close friend, a confidante. More than pleasing his sister, however, he wished he could make his mother be more cheerful.

"It sounds like you've got your hands full trying to figure out how to support your sister and travel back and forth to see your parents," I said.

"You know it! Mother is so, so . . . neurotic, unhappy. I can't *stand it*." Roy is sitting on the edge of his chair, his hands in a gripped knot.

"So what do you do?"

"I tell her, 'Stop it. Shape up!' I can't *stand it*!"

"Does that work?"

"No. But I can't help it, I just tell her to do anything other than what she's doing right now."

"And what do you hope will happen next?"

"I want her to *get happy*, take some initiative, get with the program. I can't stand seeing her so miserable." He paused, closed his eyes. "Dad was able to jolly her up. He was *funny*. He made her laugh. And now he has dementia and they don't even live together anymore. He's . . . useless. And I'm not funny." He wiped his eyes.

I think of other sons and daughters who also rail against changes in their old mothers and dads, want to go back in time, to an earlier version of Mother or Dad. Their stories and my own have led to my imagining connection and involvement within and between generations to be like Velcro: hooks reaching out on one side, loops accepting on the other. Aging and experience mess around with the size, shape and density of Velcro needed at any one time, with who does what for whom and how, in order to feel a sense of involvement. It takes a while to adjust hooks and loops, to accept that just when you get it right, life shifts things around again, not unlike parenting a young child. But this is Mother. Dad. Few anticipate how much a parent will change with age, illness, dying.

"Being around an unhappy parent can be very trying. Tell me about your visits."

Roy raised his eyes to the ceiling and scrunched up his nose for a moment. "Okay. I fly in for the weekend, get here late afternoon and go directly to her apartment. We sit, make small talk: my flight, my kids. The TV is on. I try to just sit, last about ten minutes. Then I say, 'Let's go for dinner.' We do. Then I start on her."

"What do you say to your mother?"

"'Do you want to watch a movie, Mother?' 'No.' 'Do you want to go for a walk? A drive? Do you want to go down to the lounge?' 'No.' And then I . . . yell, *'So what do you want to do, Mother?'* and she says, 'Oh, I don't know. I don't feel like doing much of anything. Maybe just sit here.' And that's when I lose it. *'Get with it, Mother.'* She cries; I can't stand it. I get up, leave her room, feel awful — what kind of a son leaves his mother in tears?" He shook his head. "I hate everything about this."

"Such amazing powerlessness — to be unable to fix what ails your mother . . ." I offered. He looked up. I continued, "In your tech work, you have moves you can make when a client has trouble with their computer. Fix it. But your mother . . ."

". . . Is a pain in the ass! Just tell me what to do and I'll do it. Anything."

"How much does this situation make you think about how the two of you connect — used to connect — with each other. You make it sound like she doesn't — in your mind — have the right to be unhappy, upset about her life."

"She can be as miserable as she wants, just not around me." Silence. Roy's eyes went wide as if surprised to hear himself say this.

A memory flew into my mind, of me stomping upstairs to the silence and privacy of the guest room in my mother's house because there was nothing I could do to make her be a happier old woman. How often I wanted to scream at her *you have so much health, family around, ample finances, friends, what is your problem?* After she died and I moved through my sixties, I saw the shifting loops and hooks of our Velcro much more clearly, wished I'd been more patient, more prescient.

"I wonder what your mother imagined life would be like in her late eighties. Any ideas?"

"She's eighty-eight, what's to imagine? It's all over, isn't it?"

"What do you think your mother thought about? Perhaps still thinks about?"

"I have no idea. No idea at all."

"I wonder what she would say if you asked her?"

"In the meantime, tell me what to do to stop her misery."

"What if you thought you couldn't fix her? What if it's not your job to fix your mother's unhappiness?"

Roy wagged his head back and forth. "What a way to end your life. You're saying she's *choosing* to be pathetic, and for me to *stay out of it*?"

"If your mother were here, I would ask her what makes her so unhappy — and that's something you might ask her, but only if you are interested in what she might tell you. I'm going to guess some of what contributes to it — not that you can fix any of it. You've told me that in the last few months your mother has lost two siblings, her husband of fifty-eight years went into a dementia care unit, the home she and your dad lived in was sold, and she moved into a retirement facility, beautiful but filled with strangers." Roy's face flushed. I stopped. Then, "That's a lot of loss. I don't know what she imagined, but I'd be surprised if she anticipated all this. How do folks in your family help each other with loss?"

"I guess we try to ignore it. And . . . this can't be ignored, can it?"

"Maybe your mother is showing you she's not ignoring it. These changes are losses for you, too, I imagine."

"Yeah."

"So if you didn't chase her — or yourself — out of being upset, what would you do instead? I don't expect you to be able to answer that right away. You may need to think about it for a while, talk with your sister, your mother. How you want to be around a mother who is sad, how you want to be with yourself when you are sad, is personal, important, often something we've not thought enough about. Having aging parents means sadness now and again; they are at the end of their life and there's a lot of change and loss afoot. For their children, too. *All* old parents and grown children are faced with this. One day, you and your children will be, too."

"I'll think about all that. Yeah. But what can I *do*? Now."

"Okay, here's a practical bit: write down everything you do to *try* to make things better, then cross off what doesn't seem to make any difference. Then stop doing those things."

"Yeah? And do what instead?"

"Not sure. Pay attention to what happens when you stop doing what doesn't work. My hunch is you'll start experimenting with what might work."

His eyes met mine. "There's no prescription, is there?"

"Don't I wish! But for starters, see if you can just *sit* with who your mother and you are at *this* time in your lives."

"This is harder than I thought it would be."

"It's a very grown-up assignment."

Not unlike Roy, sixty-five-year-old Lorraine found what she called "this mother" — the one ninety-two-year-old Greta had become — to be almost impossible to accept. Her face in a frown, she described the visits she and her sister Wendy made to the dementia unit where their mother had lived for two years as "dutiful."

"Mother would have crossed the street to get away from someone who looks like she does now, Clarissa," Lorraine said, wagging her head side to side. "Almost indecent. Embarrassing."

Lorraine said her mother had "become a witch-like creature" who refused to cut her hair, wear makeup or shoes. "Or," her eyes dropped, "underwear."

"So when you visit . . . ?"

"I've stopped trying to make conversation. It makes her eyes go wild. I walk with her a bit. Sit there. Thank God she'll let me brush her hair and even wash it." Silence. "I am totally wrung out when I leave. My sister Wendy's story is identical to mine, except Mother won't let *her* touch her hair. That seems to be *my* job. Lucky me."

"Tell me about you and your mother before she had dementia, before she lost her words."

"Ohhhh . . . She was . . . so lovely." Tears welled up in Lorraine's eyes. "Cashmere, pearls. Nails done, hair coiffed." She reached into her purse. "Here." A picture of a silver-haired woman looking directly into the camera, red lips parted in a smile, a string of pearls draped on the front of a rose-coloured sweater. "She never went anywhere without her lipstick on." Deep breath. "Most of my life, I felt lucky to get along with my mother so well; many friends didn't like their mothers so much. But Mother, Wendy and I went to the symphony, Bard on the Beach. We talked books. She was interested in my children. Then, after Dad died, she became forgetful, confused. Had to stop driving. Couldn't figure out how to put her makeup on. Wendy and I tried to keep her at home, but she wasn't safe, no matter how many caregivers we hired." Silence. "It was . . . heart-breaking."

"No wonder you miss your mother. What a rich friendship you had."

"Yes. And now . . . I don't even like her." Lorraine's eyebrows arched. "I did just say that, didn't I?"

"Yes. My sense is you find it hard to like your mother's current behaviour, to *find* the mother you used to know in there. Perhaps the good years with your mother — *that mother* — are held in a very special part of your heart. Hard as this is to put together, all of it is your mother. And her family."

Lorraine snorted. "Try this one on: Mother not only refuses to wear shoes and underwear, she's now tossing her skirts up over her backside, bending over and shouting 'Bum! Bum! Asshole.'" She looked down at her lap. Voice soft. "When I arrive, there's my mother, long white hair flying, bare bottom hanging out, walking down the hall. God."

Lorraine and her sister Wendy came to see me several times to talk about their sadness and guilt. They wanted to feel less offended, more understanding. They hadn't realized how awkward it is to grieve someone who is still alive, said it was easier to say goodbye to their dad. I asked them to bring family pictures, talk with one another and me about changes and losses.

During one session I said, "I think you're in the market for what I call new Velcro with your mother, that is, new ways to connect — *now* — even though she has dementia and you two are seniors. The Velcro 'loops' that used to fit with the 'hooks' in your relationship — the symphony, plays, books — no longer work very well. Even if your mother didn't have dementia, there would be changes that required new loops and hooks. To continue to 'grow up' a relationship — no matter how old we are — means figuring out what holds people together *now*." Both sisters stared hard at me. "And the new bonds might be a far cry from those you once enjoyed."

"The hair-brushing works," said Wendy.

"Yes, it seems to. So that's one thing."

In one recent picture, Lorraine and her daughter Pamela cuddled around a little girl, the only grandchild in the family. Lorraine said Pamela had asked her if it would be okay for eighteen-month-old Bes to meet her great-grandmother.

"I don't want to frighten that child! Mother . . . looks like a wild witch out of a dark fairy tale. What do you think, Clarissa?"

I told Lorraine there were reports that toddlers and dementia patients sometimes created connections that aren't easily understood. "Bes has no history with your mother. No comparisons. She might not be as frightened as you are. Who knows, maybe they'd be able to find something in common."

"You think Pamela and I should take little Bes to meet my mother?"

"I think so. Let Bes sit next to her mother. You brush your mom's hair as you usually do. See what happens."

Days after that Sunday afternoon, Lorraine was eager to tell me about Bes meeting her great-grandmother. As Lorraine described the encounter, her words formed pictures and sounds in my mind: I saw little Bes on her mother's lap staring with lowered eyebrows at Greta. Silent. Still. Lorraine behind Greta brushing her hair. Greta, silent, still. Eyes flickering toward the child. Then, Greta talking gibberish, sounds Lorraine had heard her mother make many times. Bes's face breaking into a wide smile and offering her own nonsense language. Greta's eyes going wide. Laughing, looking at Bes, babbling. Back and forth. Bes climbing off her mother's lap, standing in front of Greta, reaching out to touch her hair. Lorraine brushing. Bes and Greta jabbering, giggling.

How sacred, these "safe haven" moments of connection and growth with family and friends.

Lorraine sat back in her chair, smiled at me. "New Velcro?"

"Quite likely. For all of you."

I relish my time with my sons. In a few days Chandler and Larson, now forty-nine and forty-seven, will come to Vancouver for one of our annual Three Bears Retreats. Since we began this refreshing ritual a few years ago, I've come to think about it as a time when we check up on one another's grownupedness, even though we don't know we're doing just that.

In the days leading up to our Three Bears Retreats, I reflect; by the time they arrive I will have given myself a good shake to see how I am, how my life is unfolding. I will have visited shifts in my health and theirs, changes in their work and marriages, what's happening in connections with family and friends. When the three of us talk, and we do that a lot, I hope I can find words for the forces rearranging the connections in my life, for my evolving maturity. I hope they can find words for what's shaping them as they traipse through mid-life.

Years ago, I had done similar reflections before my mother visited — not that she asked me about my life in the ways I do my sons', but because I had hoped she would.

Should my mother ever have become personal, I had wanted to be ready, clear.

Ironically, Mother taught me the value of reflecting before visits with loved ones. When I was the same age as my now middle-aged sons and very interested in her and her life, late at night we sat in her living room sipping Scotch and "catching up." She found my questions flummoxing, often upsetting, and sometimes said tearfully, "I never asked my mother one good question. But you and your sisters are so full of questions." She always added that, as much as she disliked those conversations, she wouldn't miss a minute of them.

Prior to one visit when she was in her late seventies, she called me. "Please send me those questions in advance, so I can get ready. I don't spend time thinking about aging like you do."

I got it: she needed time to catch up with herself, reflect on who she was *then*.

I'm no different now than my mother was then, except I'm pretty good at generating my own questions. I need to check in with myself periodically, or I am shocked by what I've become without noticing. Grownupedness depends on taking time to acknowledge, name, find words to describe. To share then turns listeners into witnesses, other humans who validate our life by being part of it. We need friends and relatives to be like friendly talking mirrors, who remind us we are still here living our story, who help us see how we are growing into ourselves. This can be a tall order.

Exposure to what's changing in late life pushes relationships around. It should. We need to see what these connections are made of. When I got sick four years ago I knew intellectually my most special friendships needed to rearrange their Velcro loops and hooks to continue. I'd become a different friend, one with more complex needs. The changes in me — especially my more visible vulnerability and less available ever-ready strength and support for others — electrified boundaries between me and friends. Finding the way forward took time and effort that felt raw. I struggled to find words for what I felt, needed, struggled more to reach out, ask how my illness was affecting them and their connection with me.

Some of the most awkward conversations I've ever had happened with good friends during the first year of my illness. As we sat in comfortable chairs in my living room, friends looked to me to guide the conversation, but I shrugged, shook my head, insisted we feel our way forward like blind people. I'd never had cancer, been told my life was threatened. Those friendships grew sentence by sentence, climbing over one disappointment then another, until we got used to one another again, grew new superglue.

Some friends couldn't fit so well.

When I called Peggy, a long-term friend from the East Coast to tell her my bad news, there was a long silence. Because she had always said she would, I expected her to want to drop everything and come running, but instead she said. "Not you. You're the strong one." Tears. Then, a whisper: "I can't. I just can't." I assured her she didn't have to *do* anything, just be there once in a while on the phone. But she still disappeared from my life. She and I had been through so many life crises together. I still wince, find her turning-away hard to believe. Sometimes I pick up the phone to call her, but put it down, instead carry a dull ache in my heart. Now, years later, I get it: her heart-space was already littered with losses and I would be one more.

Since I became ill, I too have backed away from a few friends, loosened my attachment, usually because they kept reaching for parts of me sheared off by illness, and I couldn't regrow into someone who once had been. My efforts to teach them about the newest version of me failed, and we couldn't grow together into this new friendship. I knew — because they told me and showed me — how much they missed the old me. I told them I missed me, too.

It is not just illness that sheds our layers, exposes a more naked self. As our bodies and minds change with age, as family and friends leave and die, there are endless opportunities to get to know one's self in unabashed ways. Living long enough allows us opportunities to turn toward change with curiosity and acceptance, to become increasingly transparent as our own personal essence shines. If we choose to, we move around our most personal Velcro loops and hooks, changing our deepest relationship with our self.

When I worked with clients in their eighties and nineties who were eager to find meaning in their own aging and end of life, I imagined them as bars of soap getting slimmer and slimmer as they put themselves to good use and in the process used themselves up. In their stories and demeanours these men and women radiated with whatever they'd done a lot of — because they *had* a lot of it — be it enriched friendships; carried wisdom; complex, satisfying relationships with children, community, their god. Their attachments were integral to their sense of who they were. They worked hard to make peace with their ever-changing bodies, spent time figuring out what "aging" was all about for them. If there were such a thing as a backwards mirror, these people would look in it, see how they'd arrived where they were, and not be too surprised. Unlike peers who lived without reflection about the tangles of earlier years, they'd grown themselves forward, ended up tidy, slender, simple as bars of well-used soap.

The last time I saw my great-aunt Ruth, she was 105. We'd not seen one another in sixty years, but she smiled broadly and said, "Clarissa! How wonderful to see you!" She was in bed, leaning against soft pillows, her ice-white hair lighting up her head, wearing a cream-coloured gown. So small and thin, she looked doll-sized to me but glowed with an obvious energy. She patted the bed, wanted me to sit close, even though she said she could hear well and didn't need glasses. She touched my face, looked at my hands, said, "Yes, we are Greens, you and I." She asked about my life, told me snippets of hers: a life of engagement, loss, finding ways to embrace hard times the best she could. She was a well-worn beautiful bar of soap. As she told me she would, she lived just a few months more, then died quietly.

For me, my aging and illness have included a radical renegotiation of my relationship with my body — ever my stalwart, steady companion, ready to embrace the next social or physical challenge. I've been lucky. Until my seventies, could I have looked in my backwards mirror, I would have nodded in appreciation for all I'd done to take care of my body. Now I close my eyes and wonder, what's next? How can I be grown-up and be this sick? What arrangement with Velcro do I need, not just with friends and family, but with my body as I get to the end? Are there ways for me to end up as smooth and lovely a bar of soap as my aunt Ruth?

The first nights of my sons' recent visit seem familiar. They arrive, we crack open IPA beers, they spill their lives on the floor, talking atop one another. Their tangled marriages feel like a snarl of wool around my feet — how encompassing their lives are to them. I take in, say "Wow!" when it's called for, but I know I am not yet on their radar screens. I stay up as long as I can, then leave the two of them to be brothers together. I happily curl around pillows and go to sleep.

Two days later, the tumours in my body cause havoc, and we are forced to talk about the consequences of my body in their lives. Tears run down my face as we talk with one another in my TV room. I slump and, through the tears, tell them there's nothing I can do. My body is on a journey of its own. I am so sorry I can't be more of a "fun" mother. I feel deeply humiliated with what they have seen, heard of my body — I am very sick, and it can — and will — make their lives messy.

Silence.

Then from both of them: "It's okay, Mother. Really. We can handle it. We are handling it. We'll do whatever it takes to make all of this okay, somehow, no matter what."

In motion again: the gears of growing up together.

Acknowledgements

In no particular order...

Many thanks to The Writers Studio at Simon Fraser University for loosening and opening my language to allow my words to shape into my own voice. I am especially grateful to Miranda Pearson and Betsy Warland. In addition to my participation in her Vancouver Manuscript Intensive program, Betsy has been my teacher, mentor and friend and I owe her a special and humble thank you for her patient pacing with my wandering process toward publication.

A special thank you to my writing groups over the last forty years, especially my most recent: Leslie Hill, Ingrid Rose, Ethel Whitty and Sheila Martineau. They insisted that this book come to life and provided the wind and the wings to make that happen. Thank you also to former writing group members Eufemia Fantetti, Ayelet Tsabari, Jan Redford, Sally Halliday, Morgan Chojnacki and Karen Essex for reading and offering commentary on early drafts.

I am fortunate to have had the insight and support from many creative voices. Thank you to Louise Barker who caringly edited early drafts. And to Paul Belserene and his first-ever 1976 writing class, "Square One", which encouraged me to keep writing. I am grateful to the Pacific Coast Circle group for wanting to hear my stories read aloud, and especially to Sally Hurst for asking me to read my family stories to her at the end of her life. Hood 49, Rhizome Cafe and Take Five provided time and space for writers to read their work aloud and Joel and Florina Rogers never missed one of my readings. Thank you to my 3M friends and colleagues, Don, Bluma, David, Alex, Guy and Arshad, who were interested in my stories and gently nudged me to write, write, write. And thank you to Jo Blackmore and her competent crew at Granville Island Publishing for their skilled, quick insightful work on this book.

Over my career I have been fortunate to connect with many individuals and families who shared their personal lives and family stories, and expressed their hopes that I write down what I knew. My clients have taught me about aging and caring and growing up and I owe a tremendous thank you to the women of the original Mid-Life Daughters Workshop, Karen, Jaqui, Cindy, Pat, Andrea, Louise and Patricia, who kept meeting for seven years and wanted others to benefit from their experiences with their aging parents. And to The University of British Columbia's Continuing Studies, especially Ruth Sigal, who suggested The Mid-Life Daughters' Workshop as a program and supported it along with my other programs, The Widowed Journey and Certificate in Working with an Aging Population. Thanks also to the Pacific Coast Family Therapy Institute for showing me how story, legacy and family issues travel through generations.

I am eternally grateful to my family, especially my sisters Nancy, Casey and Suzie for their decades of interest in my writing and stories. And to my Aunt Clarissa who appointed me the "story catcher" for my family, and to my mother for being such a colourful, crispy character. And finally, to my two sons, Chandler and Larson, for reminding me often that "your stories are our stories," for being willing to be "storied" and for their unflagging interest in me as a writer.

Clarissa P. Green has spent her life exploring and teaching how family relationships are changed by aging, illness and death. In her decades-long career as a therapist, Green has helped families reconfigure their relationships and conceptions of self in the face of trauma and aging. An associate professor emerita at the University of British Columbia, Green's continuing-studies programs, The Widowed Journey and The Mid-Life Daughters' Workshop, ran for more than a decade. Green was a founder of what is now the Irving K. Barber Learning Centre, and she has received numerous teaching awards, including the Killam Teaching Prize from UBC and the 3M National Teaching Award.

Green's belief that personal experience is necessary for learning and growth developed naturally alongside a lifelong passion for storytelling. Green completed the Simon Fraser University Writer's Studio program in 2007, and her short fiction piece *The Coin* won first prize at the Vancouver International Writer's Festival in 2009. Green's numerous works have been published in anthologies, *Geist* magazine, and *The Fieldstone Review*.